The Many Blessings Cookbook

Grandma
Mabel Moses Hopping

Jane Watson Hopping

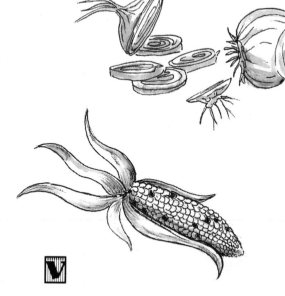

THE PIONEER LADY

VILLARD BOOKS

NEW YORK • 1993

The

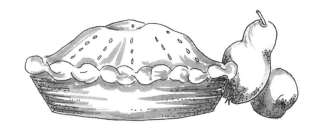

A Celebration

Many Blessings

of

Harvest, Home,

Cookbook

and

Country Cooking

Villard Books is a registered trademark of Random House, Inc.

Grateful acknowledgment is made to Contemporary Books, Inc. for
permission to reprint "When an Old Man Gets to Thinking" from
Collected Verses of Edgar A. Guest by Edgar A. Guest. Copyright 1934.
Reprinted by permission of Contemporary Books, Inc.

Library of Congress Cataloging-in-Publication Data

Hopping, Jane Watson.
The many blessings cookbook: a celebration of harvest, home,
and country cooking / by Jane Watson Hopping.
p. cm.
Includes index.
ISBN 0-679-41475-4 (acid-free paper)
1. Thanksgiving cookery.   2. Cookery, American.   I. Title.
TX739.2.T45H66   1993
641.5′64—dc20   92-46055

Manufactured in the United States of America on acid-free paper

9 8 7 6 5 4 3 2

First Edition

BOOK DESIGN BY BARBARA MARKS

TO FAMILIES LARGE AND SMALL

God, let this house be something more
Than a shelter with four corners
Standing against the four winds of the earth;
Let it be more than windows, more than doors,
More than a hearth to keep us warm.
Give it a soul! The soul of home
That reaches out beyond the walls
And, through the hearts it nurtures here
Sheds something of its own kindliness
Upon its era and its time.

God, let this house be something more
Than stout rafters and strong roof;
Let it be more than any of its parts,
And more than any single one of us
Who shall forever call it home.
May something of its mellowness and strength,
Ingrained within the structure of its sons,
Diffuse a lengthening glow upon humanity
Throughout all the years to come.

From HOME BLESSING
ELIZABETH BARR HAAS
Best Loved Unity Poems

From THE LITTLE RED RIBBON

The little red ribbon, the ring, and the rose!
The summertime comes and the summertime goes
And never a blossom in all the land
As white as the gleam of her beckoning hand!

JAMES WHITCOMB RILEY

ACKNOWLEDGMENTS

First of all, many thanks to Elizabeth Armstrong for sharing with me the delightful tale about an eventful Thanksgiving Day in the vast cattle country of Montana.

Again, I would be remiss if I did not praise the lovely decorative line art wrought by my sister Sheila, and the work of old-time illustrators, including the talented Will Vawter.

It seems to me appropriate now to name skilled poets who bring delightful imagery to the book: James Whitcomb Riley, Edgar A. Guest, Alice C. D. Riley, and Gladys M. Adams.

It is also my pleasure to list the gentle poets from *Best Loved Unity Poems*, published by the Unity School of Christianity, Lee's Summit, Missouri, among them: Elizabeth Barr Haas, R. H. Grenville, Bertha M. Russell, Mary Carolyn Davis, G. C. Constable, Clarence Edwin Flynn, Lowell Fillmore, Grace Noll Crowell, Carl Frangkiser, and Priscilla May Moore.

I am also pleased to introduce to you a handful of talented poets from the Pacific Northwest: Grace E. Hall, Alvin Reiss, Patricia Parish Kuhn, and, not least, Opal Guetzlaff, our senior poet, who is first published in this book.

As always, the support of family, friends, and neighbors is my mainstay. I also much appreciate all of the talented folks at Villard Books whose skill enhances the quality of the book; and Meg—Margaret A. Ruley—and all of the folks at the Jane Rotrosen Agency.

Again, many thanks to readers and cookbook collectors everywhere. Your kind words and encouragement fill the well and inspire yet another Pioneer Lady book.

From THANKSGIVING

Words that friendly thoughts impart,
Ties that bind us heart to heart,
Joy of human brotherhood
Spread the news that God is good.

CLARENCE EDWIN FLYNN
Best Loved Unity Poems

Contents

From UNFRAMED PICTURES

A pale shadow moon
On a dark blue velvet sky
Above a field of
Ripened yellow wheat.

A slender red-winged blackbird
Balancing on the topmost bough
Of a leaf-bare tree.

Brown wind-blown cat-tails
In a reedy slough
Beside a country road

GRACE E. HALL
Patchwork

About an Old Farmstead on Poorman's Creek

By 1959, Raymond and I had been married for nine years. We had already bought, improved, and sold three acres of sticky red earth in Orangevale, California. We had also bought an old five-acre homeplace that had a small but comfortable house on it, a good well, and an old-fashioned barn. The soil was sandy and rich. Everything grew abundantly there: potatoes, peppers, yard-long beans, an orchard, and flowers of every kind. For a number of years we were very happy on that place; our neighbors were good neighbors, and our families were close by.

Then in 1959, our little sister-in-law, who had been living with us, moved back home. Two foster children that I was caring for were moved to other locations. The children's books that I was writing weren't selling (in part because I didn't send them out). It seemed to me that the life that I had built was slipping away.

After much thought, I decided that since the children I had come to love were gone, and since I had none of my own, I would go back to college. At age twenty-nine I began my sophomore year. The intellectual

STIMULATION, MY ACADEMIC ACHIEVEMENTS, AND THE REASSURANCE OF COUNSELORS WHO INSISTED THAT I COULD WORK AT ALMOST ANYTHING THAT INTERESTED ME, GOADED ME ON TO GREATER EFFORT. THAT YEAR WAS MOST ASSUREDLY A TURNING POINT IN MY LIFE.

AT MIDBREAK RAYMOND TOOK TIME OFF FROM HIS JOB, AND WE WENT NORTH TO TAKE A WINTER VACATION IN MEDFORD, OREGON. THE TWO-LANE HIGHWAY DIPPED AND CURVED, AND SNAKED ALONG THE RIVERS, UNTIL FINALLY WE TOPPED THE SISKIYOU SUMMIT AND STARTED ON THE DOWNGRADE TOWARD ASHLAND. BELOW US WERE SOFT GRAY CLOUDS, MIST-SHROUDED MOUNTAINTOPS, AND GENTLE LATE-SUMMER RAIN.

SINCE WE DID NOT KNOW ANYONE IN THE AREA, WE STOPPED AT A REAL ESTATE OFFICE IN MEDFORD TO ASK DIRECTIONS, IN ORDER TO ORIENT OURSELVES. WE TOLD THE MAN AND WIFE THAT WORKED THERE THAT WE WERE NOT LOOKING FOR PROPERTY, THAT WE WERE JUST ON VACATION. THEY TRIED TO GIVE US DIRECTIONS AND INFORMATION. FINALLY THE MAN SAID, "LET'S TAKE A RIDE, I'LL INTRODUCE YOU TO THIS PART OF THE COUNTRY."

HE DROVE ALL THROUGH AND AROUND MEDFORD, POINTING OUT PUBLIC BUILDINGS, THE LIBRARY, COURTHOUSE, LOCAL BUSINESSES, AND SHOPPING AREAS. HE TOLD US THE AREA DEPENDED ON AGRICULTURE AND LOGGING FOR ITS REVENUE. THEN HE DROVE OUT INTO THE COUNTRYSIDE, OUT INTO THE BEAUTIFUL APPLEGATE VALLEY, THROUGH THE OLD TOWNS OF WILLIAMS AND JACKSONVILLE. HE TOOK US HIKING OVER PROPERTIES HE EITHER PLANNED TO SELL OR HAD RECENTLY SOLD, AND HE PULLED OFF THE MAIN ROAD SO THAT WE COULD WALK ALONG AND LOOK AT AN OLD PIONEER CEMETERY.

IT WAS LATE AFTERNOON BEFORE WE HEADED BACK TO TOWN. WE WERE BUMPING ALONG ON A GRAVELED COUNTY ROAD ALONG POORMAN'S CREEK WHEN WE TOPPED A RISE AND BEGAN A QUICK DESCENT DOWN INTO A LITTLE FINGERLING VALLEY CALLED GRIFFIN CREEK. TUCKED INTO THE FOLDS OF A GENTLE HILLSIDE, NESTLED AT THE FOOT OF A RIDGE OF FORESTED MOUNTAINS, WAS AN OLD HOMESTEAD, AN ANCIENT HOUSE, AND STURDY BARN, ALL IN NEED OF REPAIR. WHEN I SAW IT MY HEART NEARLY STOPPED. I KNEW RIGHT THEN THAT THAT WAS WHERE I WANTED TO LIVE FOR THE REST OF MY LIFE.

EVEN THOUGH THE PLACE WAS NOT FOR SALE, I INSISTED THAT WE CONTACT THE OWNER AND FIND OUT IF HE WOULD CONSIDER SELLING IT AND, IF SO, HOW MUCH MONEY HE WOULD WANT FOR IT. MR. MERICAN AGREED TO TALK TO THE OWNER AND FIND OUT, AMONG OTHER THINGS, ABOUT THE DEPTH AND PRODUCTION OF THE WELL, THE NUMBER OF ACRES, AND AMOUNT OF TAXES.

THAT NIGHT IN THE CABIN WE HAD RENTED, I TOLD RAYMOND THAT THE OLD PLACE WAS EVERYTHING I HAD EVER WANTED IN A HOME. HE KEPT TALKING TO ME ABOUT THE NEWLY BUILT TRACT HOME THAT WE HAD RECENTLY LOOKED AT AND REMINDED ME THAT WE HAD ENOUGH MONEY TO PAY FOR IT. I INSISTED THAT I WANTED TO LIVE ON POORMAN'S CREEK FOR THE REST OF MY LIFE IN AN ANCIENT HOUSE SURROUNDED BY TALL FIRS AND CEDAR TREES, GIANT MADRONAS, MANZANITA WITH ITS WAXY PINK BLOOMS, AND BLANKETS OF FLOWERS IN THE WOODS.

THE NEXT MORNING WE GOT UP EARLY, TALKED AND TALKED OVER A LINGERING BREAKFAST, AND THEN WENT INTO THE REAL ESTATE OFFICE. THE OWNER HAD AGREED TO LET US SEE THE PROPERTY, 120 ACRES OF OLD ORCHARD, PASTURE, WOODS, AND FORESTED MOUNTAINTOP. THE STRONG WELL PRODUCED THIRTY-FIVE GALLONS OF SWEET WATER PER MINUTE, AND THERE WAS ENOUGH ALUMINUM PIPE TO IRRIGATE A VERY LARGE GARDEN, ORCHARD, AND SMALL PLOTS ABOUT THE HOUSE. RIGHT UP FRONT WE WERE TOLD THAT THE OWNER WANTED $10,750 FOR THE PLACE, AND ASKED FOR CONSIDERABLY MORE THAN ONE-THIRD OF IT AS A DOWNPAYMENT.

BEFORE WE TALKED FURTHER OR LEFT, RAYMOND WANTED TO HIKE UP TO THE HIGH CORNER OF THE WEST PASTURE TO LOOK OUT OVER THE VALLEY. STANDING THERE, WE GLORIED IN THE SILENCE. ALL ACROSS THE VALLEY, NESTLED BETWEEN THE HILLS AND MOUNTAINS, NOTHING MOVED EXCEPT THE WHISPERING WIND IN THE TREES. THEN, FROM A DISTANCE, COMING DOWN OFF ANDERSON BUTTE, WE HEARD A CAR OR TRUCK. SOME MINUTES LATER, A CAR CAME INTO VIEW. WATCHING IT SLOWLY NAVIGATE THE NARROW GRAVEL ROAD, I KNEW THAT, WITH THE MISTING RAIN, THE SLOWER PACE OF LIFE, THE

MOUNTAINS AND FOREST, THIS OLD HOMESTEAD WAS A PLACE WHERE I COULD COMFORTABLY LIVE. COME WHAT MAY, I KNEW THAT I WOULD STRUGGLE TO MAKE THIS PLACE MY OWN AND NEVER GIVE IT UP.

SO, HAVING NO LARGE AMOUNT OF MONEY ON US, WE AGREED THAT WE COULD CUT OUR VACATION SHORT AND GO HOME TO RAISE THE $500 FOR EARNEST MONEY. WE WOULD NEED IT TO HOLD THE PROPERTY FOR NINETY DAYS WHILE WE TRIED TO SELL OUR PROPERTY IN CALIFORNIA AND RAISE THE DOWN PAYMENT.

SHORTLY AFTER WE GOT HOME, MR. MERICAN CALLED TO ASK US IF WE WANTED TO SELL THE PROPERTY FOR $15,000—THAT WOULD MEAN THERE WOULD BE A PROFIT OF NEARLY $5,000 THAT WE WOULD EARN IN ONLY TWO OR THREE WEEKS. I DREADED TO TELL RAYMOND ABOUT THE PHONE CALL, FOR FEAR HE WOULD OPT FOR THE $5,000 PROFIT. BUT I HAD MISJUDGED MY BEST FRIEND AND HUSBAND OF NEARLY TEN YEARS. ALL HE SAID TO ME WAS, "I THOUGHT WE WERE GOING TO LIVE THERE TOGETHER ON THE OLD HOMEPLACE FOR THE REST OF OUR LIVES." I MISTED UP, AND HE TOLD ME TO MAKE THE CALL AND TELL THEM THAT WE WANTED THE PROPERTY AND WOULD NOT SELL IT.

TIME PASSED, AN ENDLESS WEEK OR MORE, AND WE HADN'T RAISED $500. SO RAYMOND WENT OVER TO TALK TO LYN WYATT, AN OLD FRIEND, WHO SUGGESTED THAT WE ALL GO UP TO OREGON OVER THE WEEKEND AND TAKE A LOOK AT THE PROPERTY. HE AND NANA LOVED THE OLD PLACE. WYATT THOUGHT IT WAS A GOOD BUY AND OFFERED TO LOAN THE $500 AGAINST THE MONEY WE WOULD RECEIVE WHEN WE SOLD OUR HOUSE AND FIVE ACRES.

MUCH TO OUR AMAZEMENT, VERY SHORTLY AFTERWARD WE SOLD OUR FOUR IRRIGATED ACRES AND OUR SMALL LOOMIS HOUSE AND ONE ACRE FOR MORE THAN ENOUGH TO MAKE THE HUGE DOWN PAYMENT ON THE OLD LAND PLACE IN GRIFFIN CREEK.

THAT SPRING, WHILE I FINISHED UP MY SECOND YEAR AT COLLEGE, RAYMOND, OUR FRIEND RICHARD, AND UNCLE ERWIN HAULED MUCH OF OUR FARM EQUIPMENT AND OTHER THINGS ON AN OLD '38 CHEVROLET FLATBED TRUCK. THEY MADE

SEVERAL TRIPS OVER THE NARROW ROADS THAT WOUND THROUGH THE MOUNTAINS AND ALONG THE NORTHERN RIVERS. THEN IN JUNE, RAYMOND PUT RACKS ON THE BACK OF THE TRUCK, LOADED UP OUR CAR WITH DISHES AND PERSONAL ITEMS, AND, LAST, LOADED INTO THE TRUCK OUR OLD MILK COW, A YOUNG BULL, OUR CAGED YOUNG LAYING CHICKENS, AND MAMA CAT WITH HER NURSING KITTENS. WE STOPPED AT MY PARENTS' HOME JUST LONG ENOUGH TO SAY GOOD-BYE. THEN, THINKING OF THE CRITTERS AND THE LONG RIDE AHEAD, WE WENT ON OUR WAY. WE LOOKED BACK FOR SURE, BUT WE WERE CONFIDENT THAT OUR INSTINCTS WERE LEADING US IN THE RIGHT DIRECTION.

ON THE OUTSKIRTS OF CHICO, AN OFFICER PULLED US OVER. HE ASKED US WHERE WE WERE HEADED, AND WE TOLD HIM WE HAD BOUGHT A HOMEPLACE IN OREGON AND THAT WE WERE MOVING THERE. HE ASKED US IF WE WERE GOING ALL THE WAY TO MEDFORD WITH THE CATTLE IN THE BACK. WHEN RAYMOND TOLD HIM WE WERE, HE JUST SMILED AND TOLD US TO BE CAREFUL.

HAVING NEVER DRIVEN FARTHER THAN TO TOWN AND BACK, I FOUND THE TREK TO OREGON QUITE A TRIP. I FOLLOWED ALONG BEHIND THE OLD TRUCK, AND WE STOPPED HERE AND THERE TO WATER AND FEED THE CRITTERS. I WATCHED PEOPLE WATCH RAYMOND STOP TO WATER HIS CAT AND HER KITTENS OUT OF A THERMOS BOTTLE, AND WONDERED IF THE PEOPLE LOOKING ON THOUGHT WE AND THE CATS DRANK OUT OF THE SAME CUP. YOU COULD HARDLY BLAME THEM IF THEY DID; WE AND OUR ANIMALS DID LOOK A BIT OUT OF DATE, LIKE A LOST REMNANT FROM *THE GRAPES OF WRATH*.

BY THE TIME WE REACHED TIMBER COUNTRY WITH ITS SWEET AIR AND COOL BREEZES, I HAD A HEADACHE. SO WE PULLED OVER NEAR A COLD MOUNTAIN STREAM, WASHED OURSELVES IN THE CHILLY WATER, FED AND COMFORTED THE ANIMALS, GAVE THEM A DRINK, AND TALKED TO THEM. ONLY THEN DID WE MAKE OUR WAY DOWN THE STEEP GRADE INTO ASHLAND, THEN TO MEDFORD. WE ARRIVED AT OUR NEW HOME IN GRIFFIN CREEK JUST AT DUSK. WE IMMEDIATELY UNLOADED THE MILK COW AND THE YOUNG BULL, FED AND PATTED THEM, THEN TURNED THEM INTO A WELL-FENCED CORRAL. THEY SETTLED DOWN

IN NO TIME. WE LEFT THE CHICKENS IN THEIR CAGE, AND TURNED THE CATS LOOSE IN THE BARN.

THAT NIGHT WE ATE LEFTOVERS FROM THE DAY'S LUNCH AND CUDDLED TOGETHER ON A MATTRESS ON THE FLOOR. WE WERE EXHAUSTED NOW THAT IT WAS DONE AND A BIT UNNERVED AT WHAT WE HAD CHOSEN TO DO. ALTHOUGH WE NEEDED SOME SLEEP, WE WERE EAGER FOR THE MORNING LIGHT.

From THE RICHES OF GOD

The riches of God are manifold,
Exceeding silver, surpassing gold;
And all may take from the endless store,
Since no man lives who is really poor.
Whoever has loved or laughed or sung,
Been gay or lovely, or brave or young,
Or walked with the wind in a leafy place,
With the light of the moon on his lifted face;
Whoever has seen with his own two eyes
The new day break in the eastern skies,
Or scattered seed on the fragrant sod,
Has had a share in the wealth of God.

R. H. GRENVILLE
Best Loved Unity Poems

Introduction:
When the Frost Is on the Punkin

*E*ach year as Thanksgiving draws near, I recall our mother telling us children that Thanksgiving Day is a special day when families gather to express their solidarity and love for one another and their gratitude to the maker of us all.

Throughout the months that I have been working on this book, I have followed the rhythms of the seasons as they changed outside my office window, reveled in waning September, in the rich tapestry of October's harvest, watched cold, dark clouds give way to hazy Indian summer, and felt the chill fall winds.

Now that Thanksgiving is near at hand, I find myself remembering the gathering of my dear, old-time family, the great harvest feasts, late suppers, aunties, uncles, and cousins that finally arrived after midnight. We children were awakened to cries of "Come down! Come down! They are here!" Everyone brought with them food, bedding, and clothes enough to stay a week. We rushed down the stairs; none of us wanted to wait one more moment to start the laughter, dancing, and visiting that would fill the week to come.

During the next few days little gatherings of old women put on their best hats and coats and went to the local churches for Thanksgiving services, while their husbands stayed home to talk politics, farming, and football.

Aunt Sue's family traveled over a hundred miles to be with aging parents, aunties, and uncles, to show off new babies, and to introduce fast-growing youngsters to relatives they had never seen before. Uncle Bud, to tease the womenfolk, would swear that he had come only to sit again at the groaning family board and to see for himself if they were still the best cooks in the country.

While the women talked and planned for the Thanksgiving dinner, the men kept a close eye on the children and their games of horseshoes. Some evenings there were simple harvest suppers of fried chicken, baked potatoes, vegetables and salads of every ilk, and a pie or two. After one such supper, Old Uncle Ned vowed that he would never be able to do justice to the upcoming Thanksgiving Day dinner.

When the great day finally arrived, the trestle tables were crowded. Even so, no one seemed to mind the pressures of familial shoulders, elbows, and thighs. No one complained about little ones who cried. Young Jack and his cousins teased the girls and the young mothers who were trying to comfort babies by asking them if they were pinching the "poor little things."

Aunt Mabel took pictures with her new Kodak camera, as did other relatives. There were endless hugs and bursts of infectious laughter that passed around the table, only to stop and then burst out again with great male guffaws that settled down when the women began to bring in the steaming platters and dishes, baskets of rolls, and plates full of bread. When all was ready, young girls poured everyone's milk or coffee.

As always, one of the older men, speaking softly in a reverent voice, said grace. Everyone, religious and nonreligious, bowed their heads and closed their eyes—all except a few frisky boys of ten or twelve who gave each other knowing grins, for hadn't they heard the same words over and over at every Thanksgiving Day dinner they could remember?

While the food was being passed around the table, there was much groaning and joking. The praise ran high as men tried to outdo each other and please the cooks. Even boys tried to be a bit flowery when complimenting their aunties on a prize pie.

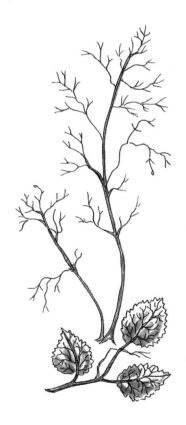

When the feasting was over, the food and dishes were put away, and everyone settled on chairs and the floor to wait for children to sing or play a piano piece that they had learned just for the occasion.

Even today, Mother talks about the feeling of belonging, of the warmth of kith and kin that spread throughout the house, leaving a silence in its wake; of how, in the quietness and peace, a grandmother or old aunt would remind the young folk that Thanksgiving is a time for serious religious thought; of how young and old, knowing well the family rituals, bowed their heads to thank God.

Today, the young families in our clan are still vital, creative, and loving. We see them often. Colleen and I make cookies together and make plans for a traditional Thanksgiving. Lisa brings rare flowers to my door, little ones who love to play on the farm. When their small hands come rattling at my door and their voices call out, "Hello, Jane Hoppin', hello!" I can hear the future calling.

From my office, I sometimes listen to all of them in my kitchen. Colleen and Lisa talk like sisters, deciding how many cans of string beans they should put up for winter, sharing recipes and talking to the children. As I listen to the rise and fall of their voices, I know that Mother is right: The old make way for the young, and life constantly renews itself.

The Many Blessings Cookbook

A Soft and Misting Rain

RAYMOND, WHOSE TEMPLES ARE GRAY NOW, AND WHOSE STRIDE IS NOT AS VIGOROUS AS IT ONCE WAS, HAS HELD OUR OLD FARMSTEAD TOGETHER FOR MORE THAN THIRTY YEARS. WITH MY HELP, HE HEALED THE FRONT PASTURE, WHICH WAS A RAPED WHEAT FIELD WHEN WE FIRST SETTLED IN GRIFFIN CREEK.

EVIDENCE OF HIS LABORS ARE ALL ABOUT US. RED CATTLE WITH WHITE FACES GRAZE IN THE GREEN FRONT PASTURE, AND WITH THEM FROLIC HUSKY YOUNG CALVES. NEW TREES HAVE BEEN PLANTED TO REPLACE THE OLD APPLE, PLUM, APRICOT, AND CHERRY TREES THAT WERE THERE WHEN WE FIRST ARRIVED. GRAPES, SOMEWHAT AGED, HAVE BEEN LINED UP ALONG THE LOW SIDE OF THE GARDEN TO KEEP THE EARTH FROM SLIPPING OFF INTO A NEARBY CREEK.

AT DUSK, HE AND I WALK ABOUT THE PLACE AND STOP TO WATCH DEER LEAP OVER PASTURE FENCES OR HIDE THEMSELVES DEEP IN AN ALFALFA PATCH. WE TALK ABOUT THE IMPROVEMENTS WE HAVE MADE DURING THE YEAR AND ABOUT THE MANY DAFFODIL BULBS WE HAVE PLANTED ALONG THE UPPER PASTURE FENCE, DAYDREAMING A BIT ABOUT THE GOLDEN BEAUTY THEY WILL BRING TO THE GARDEN AREA IN THE SPRING. WE REMINISCE ABOUT OUR CHILDREN WHO HAVE GROWN UP IN THIS FAMILY SANCTUARY, ABOUT COLLEEN, BORN IN 1962, A REAL FARM CHILD WHO LOVED TO BOTTLE-FEED THE LAMBS, AND RANDY, BORN IN 1960, WHO LOVED MUSIC AND MODEL CARS.

WE WANDER THROUGH OUR GREAT THREE-FAMILY GARDEN,

ADMIRING THE HUGE RED POTATOES, TOPS WILTED AND BROWN, THAT LIE READY FOR HARVEST. RAYMOND PULLS THE VINES ASIDE TO EXPOSE TUBERS BURSTING THROUGH THE GROUND, PUSHED UP BY VIGOROUS GROWERS THAT LIE DEEPER IN THE EARTH. THE CURLICUES ON THE GREAT SQUASHES HAVE NOT YET TURNED BROWN, A SIGN THAT THEY ARE NOT YET READY FOR PICKING. THE TATTERED LEAVES OF THE GREEN AND YELLOW BEANS, THE SMALL, INFREQUENT BLOSSOM, ALONG WITH THE STRAGGLING OVERGROWN BEANS, MARK FALL'S ARRIVAL AND THE END OF THE GROWING SEASON.

AS TWILIGHT GIVES WAY TO DARKNESS, THE AIR GROWS CHILL, AND LATE-EVENING BREEZES WORK THEIR WAY THROUGH THE GREAT MAPLE TREES ALONG THE CREEK. RAYMOND STOPS TO GATHER UP AN ARMLOAD OF FIREWOOD. WE AGREE THAT BY MORNING A SOFT MISTING RAIN WILL HAVE DRIFTED IN.

IN THE HARDWORKING DAYS THAT FOLLOW, OUR YOUNG PEOPLE DROP IN TO SEE US MORE FREQUENTLY, LINGERING TO TALK ABOUT THANKSGIVING, FAMILY TRADITIONS, AND A HARVEST SUPPER TO WHICH THEY CAN INVITE THEIR FRIENDS. SOON COLLEEN AND I WILL BE MAKING PUMPKIN, MINCE, APPLE, AND PERHAPS PEAR PIES FOR THE HARVEST HOME SUPPER AND THANKSGIVING. AND, SINCE THE SWELLING SEASON, THE PREGNANT EARTH HAS RELINQUISHED SUCH BOUNTY, WE WILL MAKE A DOZEN OR SO MORE PIES TO FREEZE AND SHARE ON COLD WINTER DAYS WITH NEIGHBORS AND FRIENDS.

LISA AND RALPH'S LITTLE ONES—RACHEL, NAOMI, AND HANNAH— FACES FLUSHED WITH EXCITEMENT, PEER INTO THE BOXES, BASKETS, AND BUCKETS OF GLEANED PRODUCE, AND THE TWO LITTLEST NAME OFF THE VEGETABLES THEY TEST WITH BABY FINGERS.

TABLE BLESSING

We thank Thee, Father, for this food
Which we receive of Thee.
Bless Thou each source from which it came:
The field, the vine, the tree.
And bless each hand that has been used
In bringing to this board

The gifts of home and far-off lands,
This bounty to afford.
We consecrate ourselves today
To do Thine own good will,
Because we know we live in Thee
Thy purpose to fulfill.

BERTHA M. RUSSELL
Best Loved Unity Poems

A Thanksgiving Blessing

WHEN RANDY WAS ALMOST THREE YEARS OLD AND COLLEEN WAS STILL A TODDLER, WE CELEBRATED OUR FIRST REAL FAMILY THANKSGIVING DINNER IN OREGON. UNTIL THEN WE HAD EITHER BEEN TOO POOR TO HAVE A REAL FEAST OR WE HAD MADE THE THREE-HUNDRED-MILE JOURNEY TO SPEND THE HOLIDAY IN THE HEART OF OUR LARGE, OLD FAMILIES.

THAT YEAR, 1963, WE HAD FINALLY ESTABLISHED FRIENDSHIPS WITH NEIGHBORS UP AND DOWN POORMAN'S CREEK: HENRY AND ALMA HUKILL, THE MADDOX FAMILY, AND THE DALTONS. AND FROM NEARBY MEDFORD, WE KNEW HERMAN AND VERA KAMPING AND THEIR CHILDREN, ALAN AND LORETTA, WHO WERE TO BECOME LIFELONG FRIENDS. WE HAD TRANSFERRED OUR GRANGE MEMBERSHIP FROM CALIFORNIA TO THE LITTLE ONE IN GRIFFIN CREEK AND HAD MADE FRIENDS THERE AS WELL. BUT MOST IMPORTANT, WE HAD TWO BEAUTIFUL CHILDREN WITH WHOM TO SHARE OUR LIVES.

BECAUSE THE CHILDREN WERE STILL SMALL AND TOOK MIDDAY NAPS, WE SAT DOWN TO OUR THANKSGIVING DINNER AT NOON. ON FESTIVE HOLIDAYS ALL THROUGH OUR FIRST YEARS IN OREGON, WE ATE WHATEVER WE HAD RAISED: BEEF OR LAMB, HOME-CANNED VEGETABLES OUT OF THE GARDEN——OR THOSE STORED FOR WINTER—— HOMEMADE PICKLES AND SAUCES AND ROLLS.

THAT DAY, WHEN THE ROLLS CAME OUT OF THE OVEN, RAYMOND SETTLED RANDY ON HIS CHAIR AND I PUT COLLEEN IN THE HIGH CHAIR, MAKING SURE THE

TRAY WAS FIRMLY IN PLACE. RAYMOND TOLD THE CHILDREN THAT HE WAS ABOUT TO SAY GRACE AND THAT THEY SHOULD BOW THEIR HEADS AND CLOSE THEIR EYES.

ABOUT HALFWAY THROUGH THE "THANK-YOU-FORS" RANDY PIPED UP, "MAMA! COLLEEN IS GETTING RIG OF THE VEGETABLES." I LOOKED UP. WITH HER TINY HAND, COLLEEN WAS EXPRESSING HER DISLIKE FOR VEGETABLES BY PICKING CARROTS AND PEAS OUT OF A NEARBY DISH AND THROWING THEM OVER HER SHOULDER ONTO THE FLOOR. WHILE I WIPED HER HANDS AND CLEANED UP THE MESS, RAYMOND LAID SLICES OF MEAT ON THE CHILDREN'S PLATES, AND BESIDE IT SPOONFULS OF MASHED POTATOES AND OTHER VEGETABLES. HE POURED THEIR MILK AND CUT A SMALL PIECE OF PUMPKIN PIE FOR EACH.

LATER, WHILE THE CHILDREN NAPPED, RAYMOND AND I STEPPED OUTSIDE ONTO THE PORCH AND FOUND A SHELTERED PLACE WHERE WE COULD SIT AND WATCH OUR SMALL FLOCK OF SHEEP GRAZING ON THE FRONT PASTURE. WE WONDERED IF THERE WAS ANY PRODUCE LEFT TO GLEAN OUT OF THE GARDENS. SHORTLY, I WENT BACK INSIDE TO CHECK ON THE CHILDREN, WHO WERE BOTH SLEEPING SOUNDLY.

AS I REACHED THE BACKDOOR, RAYMOND CALLED SOFTLY, "COME OUT AND SEE THIS DOE AND HER GROWN FAWNS!" AWED, WE WATCHED THEM MOVE THROUGH THE GARDENS, GRAZING NOW AND AGAIN ON RATTLING CORN STOCKS. WE MOVED A LITTLE CLOSER, HOLDING HANDS AND WONDERING HOW ALL THESE BLESSINGS HAD COME TO US. WE NEVER DREAMED OF GOD'S BOUNTY YET TO COME.

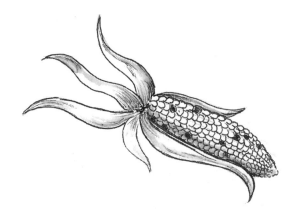

LAUGHING SONG

Sing us something full of laughter;
Tune your harp, and twang the strings
Till your glad voice, chirping after,
Mates the song the robin sings:
Loose your lips and let them flutter
Like the wings of wanton birds, —
Though they naught but laughter utter,
Laugh, and we'll not miss the words.

JAMES WHITCOMB RILEY

CHILDREN IN THE HOUSE

Sometimes a childish jingle
Flings an echo, sweet and clear,
And thrills me as I listen
To the laughs I used to hear;

And I catch the gleam of faces,
And the glimmer of glad eyes
That peep at me expectant
O'er the wall of Paradise.

From SCRAPS
JAMES WHITCOMB RILEY

A long time ago we children—my sister, I, and cousins Patty, Joan, and Billie Sue—were beloved playmates. We played together, stayed all night at each other's houses, swam in the river, and were allowed to be boisterous and silly, full of giggles and loud songs. I miss those children who used to play Farmer in the Dell and London Bridge. I miss the schoolmates, cousins all, who never let me sit alone on the schoolhouse steps with a paper lunch bag but came to find me, to enclose me and share bits of girlish gossip and their friends, if mine were sick. I miss them, yes, I miss them all.

Leeks and Potatoes au Gratin

3 POUNDS LEEKS

1 TEASPOON SALT

6 MEDIUM TO LARGE POTATOES,
    WASHED AND PARED

1 CUP MEDIUM WHITE SAUCE
    (RECIPE FOLLOWS)

½ CUP GRATED SWISS CHEESE

1 CUP LIGHT-COLORED BREAD
    CRUMBS

½ TEASPOON SALT

⅛ TEASPOON BLACK PEPPER

DUSTING OF PAPRIKA

MAKES 6 OR MORE
SERVINGS

Mary Beth, like her mother, Effie, was and is a good cook. She has copied many of Effie's best recipes, like this leek and potato dish, which for many years has been a family favorite. Effie served it with pork, while Mary Beth served it more often with roast chicken. All of us agreed it was a delightful addition to harvesttime suppers.

Preheat oven to 350°F. Thoroughly grease a 9x12x2-inch baking dish. Set aside.

Buy leeks with bright green tops and white bulbs. Cut green tops to within 2 inches of white bulbs, and peel off outside layer of bulbs. Wash thoroughly. Place leeks in a large saucepan; add 2 cups or more boiling water and 1 teaspoon salt. Cover and heat to boiling; cook until tender, 12 to 15 minutes. Drain.

Place potatoes in a large saucepan, cover with hot water, and simmer until tender when pierced with a fork. Remove from the heat, drain, and cool until they can be handled. Peel and slice. Arrange vegetables in prepared baking dish. Pour white sauce over them. Top with grated cheese, bread crumbs, salt, and pepper. Garnish with a dusting of paprika.

Bake until cheese becomes golden brown, about 15 minutes.

Medium White Sauce

MAKES 2 CUPS

¼ CUP BUTTER OR MARGARINE
¼ CUP ALL-PURPOSE FLOUR
½ TEASPOON SALT

¼ TEASPOON BLACK PEPPER
2 CUPS MILK

In a medium saucepan melt butter over low heat. Blend in flour, salt, and pepper. Stir until mixture is smooth and bubbling. Remove from heat and stir in the milk. Heat to a boil, stirring constantly. Boil and stir 1 minute more.

A Favorite Upside-Down Cranberry Meatloaf

MAKES 6 TO 8 SERVINGS

This meatloaf was quite popular in the late thirties and was brought frequently to harvesttime potluck suppers. I believe that a friend gave it first to Aunt Mabel, who shared it with her sisters and sisters-in-law, all of whom changed it a bit. We like the original recipe best and serve it often during the fall months.

¼ CUP GOLDEN BROWN SUGAR
½ CUP CRANBERRY SAUCE
2 TABLESPOONS GRATED ORANGE RIND
1 POUND LEAN GROUND BEEF
½ POUND GROUND SMOKED HAM, WITH EXCESS FAT REMOVED
½ POUND LEAN GROUND UNSEASONED FRESH PORK
¾ CUP MILK

¾ CUP CRACKER CRUMBS (OR BREAD CRUMBS)
2 EGGS, BEATEN TO A FROTH
1½ TEASPOONS SALT
DASH OF BLACK PEPPER (⅛ TEASPOON OR MORE)
2 TABLESPOONS DICED WHITE WINTER ONIONS
⅓ CUP CRUSHED NUTMEATS (OPTIONAL)

Preheat oven to 350°F. Thoroughly grease a 9x5x3-inch loaf pan. Set aside.

Spread the sugar over the bottom of prepared pan. In a small bowl mash the cranberry sauce and stir in the grated orange rind. Spread cranberry mixture over the sugar. In a large bowl combine remaining ingredients, except nuts. Shape into a loaf and pack over the cranberry mixture.

Bake until meat is firm and lightly browned, about 1 hour. Remove from oven, let meat set 5 minutes, then turn upside-down onto a platter. Spoon any glaze left in the pan onto the meat. Garnish if you wish with crushed nuts.

Green and Yellow Harvesttime Snap Bean Salad with Simple French Dressing

⅓ CUP SIMPLE FRENCH DRESSING
  (RECIPE FOLLOWS)
1 PINT (2 CUPS) FRESH OR FROZEN
  GREEN BEANS
1 PINT (2 CUPS) FRESH OR FROZEN
  YELLOW WAX BEANS

¼ CUP MINCED CHIVES
ONE 3-OUNCE JAR PIMIENTOS
RED LETTUCE LEAVES AS NEEDED
10 TO 12 LARGE PITTED OLIVES

MAKES 6 SERVINGS

If you're using beans from the garden, clean and prepare them for cooking. Prepare Simple French Dressing and chill. Meanwhile, cook beans until tender-crisp. Drain. In a medium bowl combine beans with chives and dressing. Chill for 1 hour.

Drain a second time. Add pimientos and toss. Line a medium salad bowl with lettuce leaves. Turn salad onto bed of lettuce. Arrange large olives around the edge of the bowl. Refrigerate for 15 to 20 minutes. Serve cold.

By mid- to late September the last crop of beans is being harvested. Women in our family use them in salads and ham and bean dishes, and they also serve them alone, steamed and buttered with a bit of onion. Even then there are still so many that they give them away to neighbors.

Simple French Dressing

1 TABLESPOON SUGAR
¼ TEASPOON SALT
¼ TEASPOON PAPRIKA

¼ TEASPOON DRY MUSTARD
6 TABLESPOONS SALAD OIL
¼ CUP LEMON JUICE

MAKES ABOUT ¾ CUP

Put ingredients into an attractive 1-pint, screw-top jar. Cover tightly and shake vigorously until well blended, about 1 minute. Chill in jar. Before serving, shake vigorously again, to blend ingredients.

Great-Grandma Meekins's Shoofly Pie

MAKES ONE 8-INCH PIE

In the old days, when my family lived in Missouri, women made shoofly pie for harvest home celebrations, potlucks, and other festivities that celebrated the end of the harvest season.

SINGLE CRUST PASTRY PLUS
(RECIPE FOLLOWS)
¾ CUP FINE DRY WHOLE WHEAT
BREAD CRUMBS
¼ CUP ALL-PURPOSE FLOUR
3 TABLESPOONS SUGAR
1 TEASPOON CINNAMON
¼ TEASPOON FRESHLY GRATED
NUTMEG

⅛ TEASPOON GINGER
¼ CUP BUTTER OR MARGARINE,
CHILLED
¼ CUP HOT WATER
¾ CUP LIGHT MOLASSES (OR
SORGHUM MOLASSES)
6 EGGS, WELL BEATEN
1 PINT UNSWEETENED HEAVY
CREAM, WHIPPED

Preheat oven to 400°F. Make pastry and chill. Just before filling the pie, line an 8-inch pie pan with pastry; trim and flute the edges. Prick the sides and bottom of the crust; put into the oven and bake 10 minutes, to set the crust.

Meanwhile, work together, as for pastry, the bread crumbs, flour, sugar, cinnamon, nutmeg, ginger, and butter. Set aside. Remove pastry from the oven. Combine hot water, molasses, and eggs. Pour into the pie shell. Sprinkle crumb mixture over the top.

Bake in oven until pie is lightly browned, then reduce heat to 325°F and bake 20 minutes longer. Remove from oven and set on a wire rack to cool. Serve while still warm with unsweetened whipped cream.

Single Crust Pastry Plus

½ CUP WHOLE WHEAT FLOUR
½ CUP ALL-PURPOSE FLOUR, PLUS
½ CUP FOR ROLLING
½ TEASPOON BAKING POWDER

¼ TEASPOON SALT
½ CUP BUTTER OR MARGARINE
¼ CUP COLD WATER, MORE IF
NEEDED

Sift together whole wheat and all-purpose flour with baking powder and salt. Using a pastry blender or your fingertips, work butter into the flour mixture until it resembles brown bread crumbs. Add water a little at a time, sprinkling it over the dry ingredients. Stir with a fork until dough holds together; turn onto a floured surface and shape into a ball. Chill or use immediately to line the pie pan.

SUNSET BY THE CREEK

'Tis very quiet by the creek,
The stubble field is bare,
And yellow haze is hanging like
A gauze veil in the air;
The shadows gather in the pool
Where all the riffles run
To merge in silence, calm and cool,
When their brief race is done.

A slim fish, like a silver bar,
Lies at the water's rim;
A bob-white trills his note afar,
Another answers him;
A lone bird, hidden in the brush,
Darts out and wings away,
And something in the evening hush
Moves my dumb lips to pray.

GRACE E. HALL
Patchwork

Down a Dusty Road Dappled with Raindrops and Across a Foam-Crested Creek

*W*hen we first moved onto Poorman's Creek, the road that passed by our house was narrow and graveled; along its sides were great overhanging trees, and at our driveway a maple tree that must have been a hundred years old stood in all its majesty, its canopy full and rich, shading the entire surface of the old roadway.

The creek, which almost dried up in summer, trickled through the gravel and filled small, shallow, rocky pools with clear water. Along its sheltered banks grew wild plums, tangled among the wild mint, ferns, other water-loving plants, shrubs, and trees that survived through midsummer on the creek's seepage. When our children were little, we sat with them on blankets beside the cool creek and shared a picnic lunch with their father when he came home for lunch.

In August we filled our buckets with blackberries as big as a man's thumb and wild, sweet blue plums. By late fall, fed by early rains, the creek grew deeper and deeper until it splashed over the rocky old concourse and left behind a frothy-white foam. Hovering over the water, the maple trees stood almost bare with only a few leaves hanging tenuously on their branches. Autumn was on the wane.

A Simple Citrus Marmalade

4 LARGE ORANGES

2 LEMONS

1 CUP WATER

4 CUPS SUGAR

MAKES ABOUT

4 HALF-PINTS

With a grapefruit knife or a sharp paring knife, remove the sections of oranges and lemons from the white membrane and peel as much as you can of the white membrane from the skin. Cut the orange and lemon segments in half; cut the skins in thin strips or chop into small pieces. Simmer the fruit in a medium saucepan until juice is released, 10 minutes or less. In a different pot simmer the peelings in water until they are tender. When tender, set aside to soak overnight in the cooking water.

The next morning, put the pulp in a quart fruit jar, and add enough peelings to make 1 quart. Pour into a large preserving kettle and bring to a boil. Add sugar. Boil until the jelly sheets off a spoon or until the marmalade registers 222°F on a candy thermometer. Let the marmalade sit for a few minutes, and stir the fruit into it. *(If the fruit floats and will not be stirred down, wait a few minutes more and stir again.)* Ladle into thoroughly washed and scalded half-pint jars, wipe the tops, and seal with sterilized lids and rings. Label and store in a cool, dry place. Delicious when spread with butter on Aunt Mae's Sweet Potato Rusks (page 105).

The first fall and winter that we lived on the old farmstead, I made marmalade out of citrus fruits and apples sweetened with honey, and tucked it away in a cool dry place with a few jars of blackberry jam and wild plum butter.

BETWEEN EXPERIENCE AND WISDOM

Out in the world beyond stained glass
summer walks a little slower. September twirls
through the half-open window on a half-yellow leaf.
The Sunday air is edged with cool.
Late morning brings the smell of impending school.
He tries to sing the harvesting hymn,
but the words and meaning mystify him.
When he sits in the pew, his feet almost reach the floor.
His thoughts float to meet dandelion down
drifting through the door.
He guesses he'd better pray. So he prays
for the preacher not to call on him today.
But that prayer goes greatly unanswered.
He feels his mother nudging his ribs.
He knows though not listening,
the preacher has called his name. Again. Inviting him
to pray aloud. Again. And him so young and bashful.
He has been taught that prayers must be honest.
He knows that if he does not pray
from that clear spring in the center of his heart
that God might jump down from a low-flying cloud and swat him.
So he tells the first thing that stirs in him.
"God, so far so good, thank you for what you do.
And please let me get ahold of some fishin' worms.
I know you got 'em someplace. God. Sir."
His mother nudges him again.
"Amen."

Later, at home, his mother lights into him,
and, running his bare toe around a spot on the floor,
he wishes it might have been God instead of her.
Why had he prayed for worms, she said.

JANE   WATSON   HOPPING

Why had he not prayed for peace? for health? for others?
Out in the yard Grandpa waters the grass
pretending he does not hear.
When the boy comes out in his Sunday overalls,
Grandpa says to him why had he prayed for worms.
"Cause I thought I heard God a-telling me to."
"Mmmmm," says Grandpa, thinking out loud.
"Well God, He talks to me too. He says to me
you should do what the robins do.
And where the robins do it."
The boy sees the fat, sleek robins bobbing in the spray,
pulling dinner from the diamond grass.
God and Grandpa, they help each other.
They must be friends.

Later, when the boy has gone to the creek,
the mother says to Grandpa that she couldn't see why
her boy had prayed for worms.
"Because he's a boy," the grandfather says,
"And he prayed for worms."
In the narrow moment between summer and September,
to the world beyond the world beyond stained glass,
he says between experience and wisdom,
"Because he is a boy.
God understands.
If he were a man,
he would have prayed for fish."

ALVIN REISS

A LITTLE BOY'S PRAYER

*U*ncle Ben was a feisty little boy. More than anything else he loved to tease his favorite sister Gladys (Mother) and go fishing.

One could hardly say that at seven or eight years of age he was religious; he certainly was not more so than most boys his age. However, as all the grownups began to talk about the harvest and the old women were thanking the good Lord for the blessings of plenty and praising the power of prayer, he started to take such things seriously.

He secretly told Mother, who was just a year or two older, that he was going to go to the harvest church service with Aunt Clary. Then, since there are few secrets in large families, everyone began to ask him about his unexpected interest in religious matters. After swearing on a toad's blood, Mother finally got it all out of him: He was not having much luck fishing in the stream or the pond. His face long and drawn, he told her that he'd just got to thinking about his sore luck and decided he'd ask God for a little help with the fishing and a tip or two about where to find bigger worms.

When the family found out about his practical spirituality (Mother still swears she did not let the cat out of the bag), the older, more devout members of the family were horrified at such sacrilegious behavior on the part of one of their own. Grandpa and the men who were outside smoking their pipes could barely keep from laughing out loud.

Uncle Ben stood firm: He did not let the admonitions of the older women and men sway him and he ignored the family laughter. He put on his best school clothes, washed his face, slicked up his hair, and asked his mother if he could borrow her New Testament.

When he and Aunt Clary arrived at the church, she told him that he would have to stay in his seat until the entire service was over. He did not complain. Later Aunt Clary told his mother that he had been a model child. When they left the church he shook hands with the preacher and did not pull Mary Lawson's corn-yellow braids. On the way home, Aunt Clary told him that she was proud of him and that he could take off his coat and boots when he got home.

His mother and aunts had the harvest dinner ready at one o'clock. Uncle Ben stuffed himself, then, after pie, he grabbed his fishing pole and a can for worms and ran out of the house. About one hour later, he came running into the kitchen with six fish and half a can of large worms.

Grandma Meekins told him she would cook the fish for his supper. Some of the older women sat him down and talked seriously to him about God and the good Lord Jesus, and how God heard even the sparrow fall. Eventually, he managed to escape and find his father. "Poppy, you suppose I done wrong?" he asked. "Well," his father told

him, "looks to me like your prayer's been answered." Mother always said that none of the family ever knew whether Grandpa had intervened on behalf of his middle son, but nothing more was ever said about the matter.

Through the years Mama often teased her brother a bit about his childhood conversion. But now that they are older, I hear them sharing their beliefs with each other and talking about the many blessings that have come into their lives.

Old-Fashioned Pan Fried Brook Trout

MAKES 4 SERVINGS

Great-grandma always wrapped fresh-caught fish in wild grape leaves or in herbs like wild mint. As soon as she could, she set the catch in the spring house to keep the fish cold. Just before cooking, she would lay them out to warm up to room temperature.

4 BROOK TROUT
½ TEASPOON OR MORE SALT AS
   DESIRED
SPRINKLING OF PEPPER FOR EACH
   FISH
½ CUP OR MORE FLOUR

1 CUP OR MORE FINELY CRUMBLED
   DRIED BREAD CRUMBS
1 EGG, LIGHTLY BEATEN
2 TABLESPOONS MILK
ABOUT ¼ CUP COOKING OIL

Wash the fish, then sprinkle them with salt and dust with pepper. Pour flour into a flat platter. Pour bread crumbs out onto a piece of waxed paper or foil. Beat egg to a froth; thin with milk. Dip fish first into flour, then into egg-milk wash; dip a second time in flour, then into egg wash. Roll in crumbs. Carefully lift coated fish and gently lay them on their sides in a large frying pan in medium-hot oil (when frying fish, cooking fat should not be hot enough to smoke). Fish flakes at 140°F.

Fry on one side until coating is golden brown, 3 to 5 minutes. Turn over gently so as not to break coating loose, and fry on the other side until golden, about 3 to 5 minutes. Transfer to a platter. Serve hot with or without sauce or garnish.

A Simple Lemon Sauce

MAKES ⅔ CUP

1½ TABLESPOONS CORNSTARCH
⅔ CUP BOILING WATER
2 TABLESPOONS BUTTER

1½ TABLESPOONS LEMON JUICE
DASH OF SALT (1/16 TEASPOON)

In a small saucepan stir together cornstarch and 2 tablespoons cold water to form a smooth paste. Add boiling water and cook, stirring constantly until clear, about 5 minutes. Remove from heat; add butter, lemon juice, and salt. Beat well, and serve at once over fish.

From The Gleaner

When the earth is crowned with fatness
And the yellow harvest yields
To the sickle of the reaper,
Toiling in the sunny fields;
Mark the glad contented gleaner,
Gather one by one her store
Every act of cheerful labor
Makes her richer than before.

Golden treasures, thickly scatter,
Strew the world's great surface o'er;
Man is but a humble gleaner,
Finding knowledge, seeking more.
Step by step he plods his way,
One by one his blessings rise;
He who binds his store together,
He alone is truely wise.

ANONYMOUS
Songs of Praise

That Wondrous Time of Plenty

In our area neighbors drop by to leave off a little late-season fruit or a pie for our Thanksgiving celebration. They talk awhile about the harvest being in and the winter secured. It's obvious that they know well what they are thankful for. Then they excuse themselves and go home to do small chores. Men check meat that has already been put down in crocks of brine or they light smoldering fires in the smokehouse, where the rows of hams, bacons, and pork loins hang. Then they go out to the poultry yard to check the Thanksgiving birds they have been raising.

Meanwhile, many of the farm women, who have worked in the fields to bring in the harvest, now spend time in the apple house, basement, or potato cellar, where they check for spoilage, and dream of winter pies they will make with all this stored bounty. On shelves, bottles of herbs and teas, long since dried, labeled, and stored, promise flavorful stews and meats, as well as herbal or floral teas known as tisanes that were fit for company and family alike.

Stuffed into the corners of the pantry are bags and boxes of nuts that have been put away for baking or for cracking and eating on cold

WINTER EVENINGS. NEARBY A CROCK PACKED WITH BEEF OR VENISON MINCEMEAT SITS

MELLOWING. FROM ACROSS THE ROOM THE PUNGENT AROMA OF SAUERKRAUT TANTALIZES THE

SENSES. JARS OF PICKLES, JAMS, FRUITS, AND VEGETABLES, SOME OF THEM LABELED "FOR

THANKSGIVING SUPPER," PROVIDE A COLORFUL DISPLAY ALONG THE SHELVED WALLS.

OF TARNISHED HARVEST SHEAVES

*U*ncle Bud, Aunt Sue, and their children regularly attended services at the Baptist church in the small Missouri community in which they lived. At special functions men and women of the congregation were invited to "share of themselves," which meant singing an old-time hymn, reading a bit of inspiring poetry, or speaking.

One late fall Sunday in 1936, much to Auntie's surprise, Uncle Bud stood up and told the preacher and the congregation that he had something he wanted to say. Without preamble, he spoke of the helpless, the widows and orphans, old folk, the sick, the tragedy of men out of work, and about God's love for them all. He talked on and on, his deep voice resonant and compassionate, breaking when he described the cold winter coming on and the agony it would bring with it.

Standing six foot three inches tall with his graying hair lit by the sun that streamed through the stained-glass window, he chided businessmen for not dropping their prices a little for those in terrible distress. He named farmers, Christian men in the congregation, who let their produce rot and poured their milk out on the ground before they would give it to neighbors and strangers new to the area. He called for renewal of ancient gleaning practices. And he firmly asked his assembled church brethren, "Are we, or are we not, our brother's keepers?"

He turned to the women, softly reminding them that there were children not two miles away who were hungry and cold, who needed loaves of bread, pots of soup, comfort, and kindness. When he saw that he had made them cry, he turned and walked out of the church, saddened by their distress.

Ida Louise's Braised Chicken with Vegetables

MAKES 6 SERVINGS

This chicken dish is quiet, delicious, and colorful when served with brown rice. Uncle Bud thought sweet, late-ripened red peppers would be more colorful and better tasting than green peppers. Thus Aunt Sue's braised chicken dish was always made with red bells.

½ CUP FLOUR
1 TEASPOON SALT
¼ TEASPOON BLACK PEPPER
3-POUND READY-TO-COOK
    BROILER-FRYER CHICKEN,
    CUT UP
3 TABLESPOONS BUTTER,
    MARGARINE, OR OIL

¾ CUP HOT WATER
½ TEASPOON SALT
1½ CUPS SLICED CARROTS
3 CUPS SLICED CELERY
¾ CUP FINELY CHOPPED ONION
¾ CUP CHOPPED RED PEPPER
BOILED BROWN RICE (RECIPE
    FOLLOWS)

Set out a large frying pan.

Stir flour, salt, and pepper together. Coat chicken pieces with seasoned flour. Heat fat in frying pan; place pieces of chicken in pan and brown lightly on each side. Drain off excess fat from pan; add water and salt. Cover tightly and simmer until chicken is almost done, 45 minutes to 1 hour.

Add vegetables and cook until they are tender, 20 to 30 minutes. Meanwhile, boil brown rice.

Boiled Brown Rice

1¾ CUPS WATER OR HOMEMADE
    CHICKEN BROTH (RECIPE
    FOLLOWS)
¾ TEASPOON SALT

1 TABLESPOON MELTED BUTTER OR
    MARGARINE
1 CUP BROWN RICE

MAKES 6 OR MORE
SERVINGS

In a large saucepan bring water or broth to a rolling boil. To prevent rice from sticking to pan, add salt and butter to liquid. When adding rice to liquid, stir grains in slowly so as not to disturb the boiling. Cover and cook over slow heat for 40 to 50 minutes. If rice seems to be dry, add ¼ cup or more boiling water.

When the grains have swelled to capacity, uncover the pan and continue cooking the rice over very low heat. Shake the pan from time to time until grains have separated or fluff the cooked rice with a fork. Serve as is or spoon vegetables and gravy off the chicken and over the rice.

Homemade Chicken Broth

2 QUARTS CHICKEN BACKS, NECKS,
    AND WINGS
2 QUARTS COLD WATER
4 BLACK PEPPERCORNS
1 SMALL BAY LEAF
½ TEASPOON CRUSHED THYME
3 OR 4 GENEROUS SPRIGS OF
    PARSLEY

HALF A MEDIUM ONION, PEELED
    AND CHOPPED
2 SMALL WHOLE CARROTS, PEELED
3 STALKS OF CELERY, CUT IN 3- OR
    4-INCH LENGTHS

MAKES ABOUT 1 QUART

Wash chicken parts in cold water to cover; drain. Place chicken parts in a large saucepan. Cover with cold water. Add the rest of the ingredients. Over high heat, bring liquid to a boil; reduce heat and simmer about 2½ hours or until liquid is reduced by half. Strain broth. Remove meat from chicken; return to broth if you wish to make a light soup, otherwise use only the broth (all other ingredients removed) in soups or other dishes that call for it.

Old-Fashioned Steamed Apples

MAKES 6 OR MORE
SERVINGS

*Old-time women like
Aunt Clary often
kept a bowl of
steamed apples on
hand to eat with
oatmeal on fall
mornings and with
pork at suppertime.*

10 LARGE WINTER APPLES, PARED,
    CORED, AND CUT INTO 8
    SLICES EACH
¼ CUP SUGAR

½ TEASPOON CINNAMON
¼ TEASPOON NUTMEG
1 TEASPOON VANILLA

Turn prepared apples into a large saucepan; add 2 inches hot water. Cover and simmer until apples are tender. Stir in sugar, cinnamon, nutmeg, and vanilla. Steam 3 to 5 minutes longer to blend seasonings. Turn off heat; remove cover. Serve hot or cold with or without heavy cream spooned over them.

Harvard Beets

*This old-time side
dish has been served
with roast beef, pork,
or fowl. Effie
preferred it with
pork, while Aunt Sue
served it with a
tender beef roast.
Mama always cooked
carrots and potatoes
with her roast, and
thus more than one
delicious winter
vegetable graced the
table.*

1½ CUPS COOKED BEETS, DRAINED,
    SKINNED, AND DICED
    (RESERVE ¾ CUP LIQUID FROM
    THE BEETS; IF NECESSARY ADD
    ENOUGH WATER TO MAKE
    ¾ CUP)
2 TABLESPOONS SUGAR

1 TABLESPOON CORNSTARCH
½ TEASPOON SALT
A FEW GRAINS PEPPER
3 TABLESPOONS CIDER VINEGAR
2 TABLESPOONS BUTTER OR
    MARGARINE

Set beets aside.

In a medium saucepan mix together sugar, cornstarch, salt, and pepper. Stir in reserved beet liquor and vinegar. Bring to a boil, stirring constantly. Add beets and butter or margarine.

Again bring to a boil. Stir gently and constantly; simmer 8 to 10 minutes.

Each year in late October or early November, the women begin the baking so there will be enough pies ready on an allotted day to share with widows, orphans, and old folk who live alone in the community.

Ida Louise and Effie are especially thoughtful and kind. I can't help but think they find kindred spirits in each other. They seem to share the knowledge that when they get older they too will look forward to holiday baked goods brought to them by the laughing and loving young women of the family. It's as though they anticipate receiving the very kind of joy they are so eager to give now.

Honey Pecan Pumpkin Pie

SINGLE CRUST PASTRY PLUS (PAGE 12)
1½ CUPS COOKED OR CANNED PUMPKIN
⅔ CUP GOLDEN BROWN SUGAR
1 TEASPOON CINNAMON
½ TEASPOON FRESHLY GRATED NUTMEG
½ TEASPOON GINGER

½ TEASPOON SALT
¼ TEASPOON GROUND CLOVES (OPTIONAL)
2 EGGS, BEATEN TO A FROTH
1½ CUPS MILK
½ CUP HEAVY CREAM
1 CUP PECANS, CHOPPED
¼ CUP HONEY

MAKES ONE 9-INCH PIE

This delicious pie has always been Aunt Sue's favorite. Through the years she has shared her recipe and taught all of the girls in the family how to make it.

Preheat oven to 425°F. Line a 9-inch pie pan with pastry.

In a large bowl combine pumpkin, brown sugar, cinnamon, nutmeg, ginger, salt, and cloves. Stir until sugar is dissolved. When thoroughly blended, pour eggs, milk, and heavy cream into the pumpkin mixture. Stir until smooth.

Bake pie shell in 425°F oven for 25 minutes to set the crust. Remove from oven and fill with pumpkin mixture. Reduce oven temperature to 350°F and bake until a knife blade comes out clean when inserted, 40 to 50 minutes.

When pie is done, turn off oven and transfer pie to a wire rack to cool. When thoroughly cool, sprinkle chopped pecans over the entire surface and pour warmed honey over pecans.

From The Joy of Giving

I shared my crust with a poorer one,
And the crust which had seemed but a bit of bread
When one would eat was a glorious feast
When shared with another instead.

My gift was poor, but was of my best,
I had given myself when I gave my food.
But the joy that came transfigured all,
And I felt that God was good.

GLADYS M. ADAMS
(AGE 16)
St. Nicholas

AUNTIE AND ME

Mother's friend Ethel, whom I called Auntie, was a thrifty woman who encouraged all of the newly married girls, including myself, to be frugal. "Waste not, want not!" she would tell us, and "A careless woman can throw more [food] out the backdoor than both man and wife can bring in the front."

She taught her children to trim the meat off their chops, steaks, or chicken and put the bones on the "bone plate." When she roasted a turkey, leg of lamb, or a piece of pork or beef for company dinner, she always boned and sliced the meat in the kitchen before serving it on her great stoneware platter. After the meal, whether it was a Sunday dinner or harvest celebration, she put all the bones and trimmings, excluding the fat, into a large stockpot to be cooked off later that day.

When the broth was finished, she removed the meat from the bones, returned it to the broth, and discarded the bones. Uncle Joe would then carry the hot kettle of broth out to the springhouse to chill overnight. Late the next day, he would bring the soup pot back to the kitchen. Auntie would lift the hardened fat off the top of the broth and fill the pot with onions, potatoes, carrots, and celery if she had it. She would throw in a turnip or two out of the garden, salt, pepper, and a blend of secret herbs and spices, then simmer the whole until the vegetables were tender.

On such evenings it seemed the word that there was soup simmering on the stove got around. Several cousins would drop in "just to visit," and a neighbor or two would stop by to see if Uncle Joe and Aunt Ethel needed any help with the end of the harvest. All were invited to stay for supper. Soon the table was crowded; hungry men, women, and children sat elbow to elbow. Everyone was handed deep, steaming bowls of soup and platters of buttermilk biscuits so light they almost lifted off the plate. These platters were followed by a crock of freshly churned butter. On the back of Auntie's old wood-burning cookstove, the soup pot steamed, the aroma wafting here and there, coaxing men and boys to have a bit more soup to go with their biscuits.

Auntie would almost always remember that she had forgotten to bring out a jar of her wild blackberry jam to go with the biscuits. And, to everyone's delight, she would send one of her girls in after it. With these suppers Auntie made it clear that we didn't have to forgo taste in our pursuit of frugality.

A Hearty Supper Soup

MAKES ABOUT 24
SERVINGS

*Auntie used any
combination of
vegetables she had on
hand in this old-time
soup. She always
served it with chunks
of homemade bread
or with a great
platterful of her light
whole wheat
buttermilk rolls.
Often she treated
family, friends, and
neighbors to a little
dessert of fresh
gingerbread when
they had had their fill
of this hearty dinner
fare.*

4 QUARTS STOCK (RECIPE
   FOLLOWS)
3 TABLESPOONS BUTTER OR
   MARGARINE, MORE IF NEEDED
3 LARGE OR 4 MEDIUM ONIONS,
   PEELED AND CHOPPED
3 CUPS OR MORE CHOPPED CELERY
½ CUP WATER
3 CUPS OR MORE CARROTS,
   PEELED AND DICED

3 CUPS OR MORE POTATOES,
   PEELED AND DICED
4 CUPS CANNED OR FRESH
   TOMATOES
3 CUPS OR MORE STRING BEANS,
   PEAS, OR LIMA BEANS
SALT AND PEPPER TO TASTE

Before assembling the ingredients for soup, set out a large (2-gallon) covered pot and prepare stock in it.

Melt butter in a large frying pan, add onions and celery, and sauté until both are soft and onions are yellow. Turn into the stock kettle. Rinse the frying pan with ½ cup water and pour that into the soup pot. Add carrots, potatoes, tomatoes, and string beans (or peas or lima beans). Add salt and pepper to taste. Cover the pot. Set over high heat and bring to a boil. Reduce heat to medium and simmer until vegetables are done. Serve with Homemade Croutons (page 57) or Whole Wheat Buttermilk Rolls (page 141).

Stock

MAKES 4 QUARTS STOCK

LEFTOVER BONES FROM STEAK,
   CHOPS, OR ROASTS WITH
   SCRAPS OF MEAT, OR A RAW
   SOUP BONE OBTAINED AT A
   BUTCHER SHOP
4 QUARTS COLD WATER

1 TABLESPOON SALT
1½ TEASPOONS PEPPER
¼ CUP MINCED ONION
HERBS OF YOUR CHOICE (BAY
   LEAF, PARSLEY, THYME)

In a large (2-gallon) covered pot, combine all of the ingredients in the cold water. Cover. Set over high heat and bring to a boil. Turn heat down to medium and simmer for 2 hours. Set aside to cool. When cool, remove fat from the surface of the stock. Remove bones and strain stock through a sieve. Measure and add enough water to yield 4 quarts stock.

Homemade Whole Wheat Crackers

1 CUP WHOLE WHEAT FLOUR
1 CUP ALL-PURPOSE FLOUR
½ TEASPOON SALT

¾ CUP MILK
½ CUP MELTED BUTTER
1 TABLESPOON HONEY

MAKES 3 DOZEN

Preheat oven to 350°F. Lightly grease the back of a large baking sheet.

In a medium mixing bowl combine dry ingredients. Make a well in the center. In a small bowl blend milk, melted butter, and honey; stir until honey has dissolved; pour into the well. Blend ingredients together until a ball of dough is formed. Put about half of the dough in the center of the baking sheet; using a rolling pin, roll until dough has stretched out thin (it should be as thin or thinner than piecrust). Trim extra dough off the edges of the baking sheet. With a sharp knife, cut dough into 1½-inch squares, using a ruler if necessary to get the crackers evenly squared up.

Bake until crackers are firmed up and lightly browned, 25 minutes. Remove from oven; transfer crackers while still warm to a platter or cooling rack. When cool, store in an airtight container.

In the thirties, Effie began to talk to her friends and relatives about the need to change from white flour to whole wheat. It wasn't much of a change for most of the women who had grown up on farms where homegrown wheat, ground at the mill, was part and parcel of their winter supplies.

Girls and women baked whole wheat bread, whole wheat pastry, and some, like Effie, learned to make crackers.

One Egg Gingerbread

MAKES 9 SERVINGS

The men in Auntie's family all loved gingerbread for an after-supper treat to go with piping hot coffee or tea. She baked it in a huge pan, making enough to feed her enormous family and everyone who might drop in.

This recipe makes just enough gingerbread for my small family and a bit more for lunch the next day.

2 CUPS ALL-PURPOSE FLOUR
2 TEASPOONS BAKING POWDER
¼ TEASPOON BAKING SODA
2 TEASPOONS GINGER
1½ TEASPOONS CINNAMON
½ TEASPOON SALT
⅓ CUP BUTTER OR SHORTENING, SOFTENED AT ROOM TEMPERATURE

½ CUP SUGAR
1 EGG, WELL BEATEN
⅔ CUP MOLASSES
¾ CUP BUTTERMILK
SPICED WHIPPED CREAM (PAGE 97) (OPTIONAL)

Preheat oven to 350°F. Thoroughly grease and flour an 8x8x2-inch cake pan. Set aside.

Into a medium bowl sift flour three times with baking powder, baking soda, spices, and salt. In a large bowl cream the butter until light. Gradually add sugar; continue to cream until mixture is fluffy. Stir in the egg and molasses. Add flour mixture a little at a time, alternately with the buttermilk; beat well after each addition. When batter is smooth, turn into prepared pan.

Bake until well risen and light in texture, 50 minutes, or until done. (To test doneness, insert a toothpick into the center of the top; if it comes out clean the gingerbread is done.) Set pan on a wire rack to cool. Serve in squares while still warm, plain or with a dollop of Spiced Whipped Cream.

Of Dancing Flames, Confidences, and Blessings Rare

WHEN I WAS SMALL AND LIVED ON THE OLD HUBBARD PLACE, WE HAD ORCHARDS, GRAIN FIELDS, PRODUCE GARDENS, CATTLE, HOGS, SHEEP, AND HUGE WORKHORSES.

THE HOUSE WAS THE LARGEST WE HAD EVER LIVED IN. THE LIVING ROOM HAD A MONSTROUS FIREPLACE AND LARGE WINDOWS. THE FRONT PORCH—SOME MIGHT CALL IT A VERANDA—WAS WITHOUT PILLARS, RAILINGS, STEPS, OR BANISTERS. IN SUMMER MY SISTER, SHEILA, AND I PLAYED FOR HOURS ON THE PORCH, AND IN WINTER IT SHELTERED US FROM STORMY WEATHER.

AFTER THE FALL HARVESTS WERE IN, THE PACKERS GONE FROM THE FRUIT SHEDS, THE WINTER BUTCHERING DONE, AND ALL THE CANNING AND DRYING OF FRUITS AND VEGETABLES FINISHED, AUNT MABEL, AUNT HATTIE, AND MY COUSINS JOAN, PATTY, AND BILLIE SUE CAME OVER ON RAINY DAYS TO VISIT AND HAVE LUNCH.

From THE OLD TRUNDLE-BED

O the old trundle-bed! O the old trundle-bed!
With its plump little pillow, and old-fashioned spread;
Its snowy-white sheets, and the blankets above,
Smoothed down and tucked round with the touches of love;
The voice of my mother to lull me to sleep
With the old fairy stories my memories keep
Still fresh as the lilies that bloom o'er the head
Once bowed o'er my own in the old trundle-bed.

JAMES WHITCOMB RILEY

AFTER WE HAD ALL EATEN, MOTHER AND HER SISTERS WOULD SETTLE DOWN BY THE FIREPLACE TO TALK. WE CHILDREN SAT ON QUILTS ON THE FLOOR WHERE WE PLAYED PAPER DOLLS OR HOUSE. GRANDPA WOULD COME IN REGULARLY TO STOKE THE FIREPLACE AND TALK WITH HIS DAUGHTERS. SOMETIMES HE WOULD BRING US A LITTLE BUCKET OF OVERRIPE FIGS, THE LAST OF THE SEASON, OR A FEW APPLES THAT HUNG LATE ON THE BOUGH.

AS THE AFTERNOON WORE ON, MAMA, AUNT HATTIE, AND AUNT MABEL TOLD EACH OTHER SECRETS ABOUT NEW BABIES TO BE BORN INTO THE FAMILY. AUNT HATTIE TOLD US THAT A STORK WOULD BRING THEM. AUNT MABEL TOLD US THAT WHEN WE GOT A LITTLE OLDER SHE WOULD TELL US WHERE BABIES REALLY CAME FROM.

ONE DAY, WHEN WE WERE ALL SITTING NEAR THE FIRE, OUR FRIEND MARY CAME OVER—SHE LIVED JUST A FARM AWAY—AND SHE SHOWED US HER NEW BABY, ALL

JANE WATSON HOPPING

WRAPPED UP IN A BLANKET. WE LITTLE GIRLS WERE ENTRANCED WITH ITS TINY HANDS AND FEET AND ITS ROSEBUD MOUTH. MARY TOLD US HER BABY'S NAME WAS RUTH. LATER, WHILE THE WOMEN TALKED, MARY UNBUTTONED HER DRESS, HELD THE BABY TO HER, AND HELPED IT NURSE. WE LITTLE GIRLS WERE SURPRISED AND DELIGHTED. WE COULD HARDLY BELIEVE THAT BABIES NURSED LIKE LAMBS AND BABY CALVES.

ALL PLAY STOPPED, CONVERSATION SHIFTED TO NEW BABIES AND NAMES THEY MIGHT BE GIVEN. THE WOMEN DISCUSSED NURSING AND HANDLING, BURPING AND OTHER BITS OF BABYHOOD LORE. AS THE AFTERNOON WANED, MARY SAID SHE HAD TO GO HOME. WE ALL HATED TO SEE HER LEAVE WITH PRECIOUS LITTLE RUTH.

OF LAMBS AND SAILING SHIPS

My friend Alvin Reiss often recalls trips into the woods with his mother to gather pecans. Fondly he reminisces about sitting beside her on the ground, searching the swiftly changing clouds for shapes: old men with pipes, women with wildly flowing hair, lambs and sailing ships, clouds and more clouds on their way, scudding across the sky.

Oh, how they pondered about the wonders of the heavens and rejoiced at the miracles on the earth about them.

From LIMBS HIGH ABOVE US

You and I on gray fall days
when Dad was away at work
would walk through the woods
near our Oklahoma house,
through brown leaves, down
from their productive summer,
down, returning to the memory of earth.
I, your child, carried a one-pound sugar sack,
cloth, not knowing that you gave me that

knowing that I could fill it
while you filled the five-pound cambric flour sack
with the pre-winter bounty dropped
from pods of astonished turtle mouths
singing their silent chorus
from tree limbs high above us
against the flat gray face of the sky.
In childish confidence I knew I could touch it,
that sky, because it lay
right on top of the treetops, and the nuts fell
from the treetops to the ground, and I
could walk on top of the ground.
I could go up if they could come down.
The trees were so high. But the sky was so low.

You taught me to take only those which fell to us; those that were given us
by the wind that swayed the trees.
We should never flail the trees, you said,
never beat them with their broken limbs.
Pecans pried from their protective pods
are bitter, you said, and I learned, later,
for myself.
But those that fell in their time,
after their measure of nights and days and seasons, were sweet.
They emerged from their cracking shell
well formed and whole.

We took them home to let them dry
in a box in the corner of the kitchen.
In the winter, by the heat of the woodstove,
we opened them and let them listen
to stories of our family; stories of army,
and weddings, and babies growing
inside the young women who had married in,

summer brides of our cousins in uniform.
We saved their centers on kitchen shelves,
in Ball mason jars. Then we brought them
to the winter feasts of our gathered family.
They were always the last treat
on our table of generations, warm and sweet,
the center and substance of homemade pie.

They came from the seasons, the earth the sky
to be a part of us, and they will be
until, in our time, we fall from the tree of memory
into waiting hands.

ALVIN REISS

Ella's Southern Sausage Casserole

MAKES 4 OR MORE
SERVINGS

*This easy-to-make
supper dish is
delicious when
served with Cabbage,
Apple, and Carrot
Salad with Ella's
Cooked Salad
Dressing (page 94)
and homemade rolls
or Aunt Mae's Sweet
Potato Rusks (page
105).*

4 LARGE SWEET POTATOES, BAKED
1 POUND LEAN, UNSEASONED PORK
    SAUSAGE (SEASON AT HOME
    WITH 1 TEASPOON SALT, ½
    TEASPOON BLACK PEPPER,
    AND ½ TEASPOON NUTMEG)

4 LARGE BAKING APPLES
    (STAYMANS OR WINESAP),
    CORED, PEELED, AND CUT INTO
    THICK SLICES
1 TEASPOON SALT
1 TEASPOON NUTMEG
LIGHT BROWN SUGAR AS DESIRED

Preheat oven to 350°F. Thoroughly grease and set out a 9x12x2-inch baking pan.

    Peel baked sweet potatoes and cut into thin slices. Place half in the bottom of prepared pan. Cover with sausage shaped into 4 to 6 patties. Arrange apple slices over sausage. Sprinkle with salt and nutmeg. Cover with remaining potatoes. Brush with water, then sprinkle brown sugar over top of casserole dish.

    Bake until potatoes, meat, and apples are tender when pierced with a fork, 45 minutes to 1 hour.

Broccoli with Nutmeg Butter

MAKES 6 OR MORE
SERVINGS

*Late in the fall, when
rains refresh the
earth, broccoli
survivors of the
summer come into
their own and the
great green plants
abundantly produce
sweet, tender heads.*

2 POUNDS FRESH BROCCOLI
½ TEASPOON SUGAR
1 TEASPOON SALT

3 TABLESPOONS BUTTER OR
    MARGARINE
¼ TEASPOON NUTMEG
¼ TEASPOON PEPPER

Remove large leaves and lower tough ends of the stalks. If large, split in half lengthwise or cut into quarters. In a large saucepan boil uncovered in 1 inch or more water for 5 minutes with sugar and salt. Cover and cook until tender, 15 to 20 minutes. Melt butter and brown lightly. Add nutmeg and pepper.

    Drain broccoli and turn onto a platter. Pour butter over top.

Delicious Sweet Carrot Pickles

15 OR 20 TENDER YOUNG CARROTS   **2 CUPS CIDER VINEGAR**
2 CUPS GRANULATED SUGAR   **2 TABLESPOONS PICKLING SPICE**

In a large saucepan, boil carrots until skin slips. Remove skins; slice carrots or leave whole. Drain. Pour combined sugar and vinegar boiling hot over carrots (double batch or syrup if needed). While still hot add pickling spice. Let stand overnight. Turn into a large gallon jar that has a tight lid. Store under refrigeration.

Or process in sterilized pint canning jars sealed with a new sterilized lid and ring. Simmer in boiling water bath for 15 minutes.

Uncle Ned always planted a spring and a fall garden in addition to his midsummer garden. "That keeps vegetables comin' most of the year," he'd say. Sometimes the women helped him put up pickled carrots. Most of the time he made them up himself and put them in a large gallon jar. When his carrot pickles had all been eaten, he would start a new batch.

MORNING GREEN TO TWILIGHT GRAY

Their lives wound morning green to twilight gray,
a pre-war soldier and his country girl,
Army khaki and Oklahoma clay.
How fast warm and winter years did whirl,
as dust behind a '30s Pontiac;
a home in tune with summer radio:
Al Jolson, Kay Kyser, ourselves turned back.
Through children, grandchildren, their life's bloods flow
toward new mornings they will never see
from their twin graves in Oklahoma earth.
Yet they loved once, true and well. Let them be
for this a testament to human worth.
Aunt Essie sleeps, a cross above her head.
The Star of David shines on Uncle Ed.

ALVIN REISS

Delicious Pumpkin Nutbread

MAKES 2 LOAVES

When our friend Alvin Reiss lived with his parents in Oklahoma, in the fall he and his mother picked up wild pecans to use in winter pies and other recipes. In Missouri, our family, like his, picked up wagonloads of pecans and other wild nuts and berries on the bottomlands of the Osage River, some of which sold; the rest shared or stored away for winter use.

Mother remembers that her share of the nut money often bought new shoes and other clothes for school.

3 CUPS ALL-PURPOSE FLOUR

1 TEASPOON BAKING POWDER

1 TEASPOON BAKING SODA

1 TEASPOON SALT

1 TEASPOON CINNAMON

1 TEASPOON GROUND NUTMEG

½ TEASPOON GINGER

¼ TEASPOON CLOVES

4 EGGS

2 CUPS GOLDEN BROWN SUGAR, FIRMLY PACKED

2 CUPS COOKED PUMPKIN, STRAINED, OR CANNED PUMPKIN

1¼ CUPS MELTED BUTTER

1 CUP CHOPPED NUTS (WALNUTS OR PECANS PREFERRED)

Preheat oven to 350°F. Thoroughly grease and flour two 9x5x 2¾-inch loaf pans.

Into a medium bowl sift flour with baking powder, baking soda, salt, and spices. In a large bowl beat eggs until thick; add sugar gradually. Whip in the pumpkin and melted butter. Gradually stir dry ingredients into the egg-pumpkin mixture, beating well after each addition. Fold in the nuts, then pour batter into prepared loaf pans.

Bake until well risen, golden brown, and firm to the touch, or until a toothpick inserted into the center comes out clean. Remove from oven and cool for 10 minutes in pans set on a wire rack. Turn out of the pans; set loaves top side up. Serve either still warm or cold.

ABOUT FIFTY GOLDEN YEARS

*O*ld-time marriages were working partnerships from the start. Some were blessed, others lacked that special glow that shone around a man and woman bound together spiritually for life. The majority of people still farmed for a living. Days were often long and sometimes filled with drudgery, but men and women seemed to take pleasure in their accomplishments, each holding up their end of the bargain. Men cleared pastures of stumps and hauled rocks from the fields, tended cattle, hogs, sheep, and horses. Women milked cows, made butter, and raised chickens for meat and eggs. They cleaned the house and washed the clothes on a scrub board or on a rock in the creek. The wives also bore and tended large families of children for whom they cooked both early in the morning and late in the evening.

When twilight fell and the small children were in bed, men and boys were still out in the barn doing chores—feeding cattle, checking the foals, and more. During this rare quiet time, the women hung their cares up with their aprons on a peg on the wall and settled into their favorite chairs to dream dreams and forget the burdens of the day. Many were pious, and with black Bible in hand, they often lifted their grateful hearts in songs of comfort and joy, old-fashioned songs of praise like "Wonderful Peace":

Peace! peace! wonderful peace,
Coming down from the Father above;
Sweep over my spirit forever, I pray,
In fathomless billows of love.

Or songs of worship like "God Leads Us Along," which dates back to 1903:

In shady green pastures,
So rich and so sweet,
God leads His dear children along;
Where the water's cool flow bathes
the weary one's feet,
God leads His dear children along.
Some thro' the waters, some thro' the flood,
Some thro' the fire, but all thro' the blood;
Some thro' great sorrow,
but God gives a song;
In the night season and all the day long.

And thus, men and women who pitted their strength together to face tasks too great for one alone conquered battles of life.

Aunt Essie's Roasted Capon with Cornbread Stuffing

MAKES 8 TO 10
SERVINGS

By late fall, large capons—castrated roosters—weighed five to eight pounds. On the farms women were serving these tender, good-flavored birds at potlucks, harvest suppers, and

CORNBREAD STUFFING (RECIPE
  FOLLOWS)
5- TO 8-POUND CAPON
¼ CUP MELTED BUTTER

2½ TEASPOONS SALT
1 TEASPOON BLACK PEPPER
1 TEASPOON OREGANO OR THYME
GARNISH AS DESIRED

Preheat oven to 325°F. Set out an open, shallow roasting pan that has a rack. Make the stuffing just before chicken is prepared for roasting.

Wash capon and pat dry. *Since bird is to be stuffed, do not salt the cavity.* First, fill wishbone area with stuffing; fasten neck skin to back with skewers. Fold wings across the back with tips touching. Do not pack cavity; lightly fill as stuffing will expand while cooking. With a string or light cord tie the drumsticks to the tail.

Lay bird on the rack in the roasting pan, breast side up. Brush with melted butter; salt and pepper lightly; sprinkle on herbs. Do not cover or add water. Roast until thickest parts are tender to the fork and drumstick meat feels soft when pressed between fingers, 2½ to 3½ hours. When done, remove from oven; let sit about 10 minutes, then spoon stuffing into a serving bowl. Carve capon in the kitchen, arrange on a platter, and garnish, or put capon on a platter and carve bird at table.

all sorts of other occasions. Our mother always raised a few for their meat, which was a favorite at special dinners, autumn birthdays, and such.

Northern Cornbread

1½ CUPS ALL-PURPOSE FLOUR

¾ CUP YELLOW CORNMEAL

¼ CUP SUGAR

4½ TEASPOONS BAKING POWDER

1 TEASPOON SALT

1 EGG, BEATEN TO A FROTH

⅔ CUP MILK

⅓ CUP MELTED BUTTER OR
  MARGARINE, PLUS 1
  TABLESPOON FOR GREASING
  THE SKILLET

Preheat oven to 435°F. Grease a casserole or heat a heavy iron skillet enough to melt 1 tablespoon of butter in it.

In a medium bowl combine flour, cornmeal, sugar, baking powder, and salt. Mix thoroughly. In a small bowl, put the beaten egg, milk, and melted butter; stir together until smooth. Pour the liquid into flour mixture, all at once, stirring only enough to dampen the dry ingredients. Batter should be lumpy—overstirring makes tunnels in the bread. Turn the batter into greased pan, spread it out evenly, and bake until well risen, golden brown, and firm to the touch, 25 to 30 minutes. When done, turn out upside-down and break into pieces as needed for Cornbread Stuffing.

Cornbread Stuffing

ENOUGH TO STUFF A 5-
TO 8-POUND BIRD. FOR
MORE STUFFING,
DOUBLE THE RECIPE.

*This recipe calls for
winter-keeping
onions, which, when
kept in a warm
storeroom, do not
sprout (send up
greens) as readily as
do moister salad and
sandwich onions,
which begin to sprout
and spoil shortly after
harvest.*

¾ CUP MINCED YELLOW OR WHITE
WINTER-KEEPING ONION
1½ CUPS CHOPPED CELERY STALKS
AND LEAVES
1 CUP BUTTER OR MARGARINE
5 CUPS SOFT GOLDEN EGG BREAD
CRUMBS

4 CUPS NORTHERN CORNBREAD
CRUMBS
2 TEASPOONS SALT
1½ TEASPOONS CRUSHED OREGANO
½ TEASPOON BLACK PEPPER

In a large skillet, cook and stir onion and celery in butter until onion and celery are tender. Add 2 cups or more hot water to hot vegetables and butter. Turn off the heat. In a large bowl blend together egg bread crumbs and cornbread crumbs, salt, oregano, and pepper. Add celery-onion mixture to bread crumbs and stir well together. Stuff large chicken just before roasting. If capon is smaller (5 pounds), either make a smaller batch of stuffing or bake the remaining stuffing in a greased casserole.

Harvesttime Fruit Salad

MAKES 6 TO 8
SERVINGS

*When the fall rains
come, walnuts split
their outer skins and
fall, light and tan, to
the ground at the base
of the tree on which
they grew. Apples of
every variety are in
plentiful supply, as is
celery.*

1 CUP CHOPPED WALNUTS
4 CUPS APPLES, WITH OR WITHOUT
PEELING, CUT IN QUARTERS
AND SLICED THIN

1½ CUPS CHOPPED CELERY
6 TO 8 RED LETTUCE LEAVES
DELICIOUS SALAD DRESSING
(RECIPE FOLLOWS)

In a medium bowl combine walnuts with thinly sliced apples. Add celery. Add enough Delicious Salad Dressing to moisten the salad. Just before serving, spoon salad mixture onto salad plates covered with washed, drip-dried, crisp lettuce leaves.

Delicious Salad Dressing

1 CUP THICK CULTURED SOUR
   CREAM
1 TABLESPOON SUGAR
1 TABLESPOON LEMON JUICE,
   STRAINED

PINCH (⅛ TEASPOON) SALT
SPRINKLING OF WHITE PEPPER

MAKES 1 CUP

In a small bowl, combine sour cream, sugar, and lemon juice. Season with salt and pepper to taste. Chill.

The women in our family make what they call fruit salad, dress it with homemade dressing, and serve it on a crisp red lettuce leaf.

Southern Style Sweet Potatoes

4 FULL-FLESHED, MEDIUM SWEET
   POTATOES, BOILED
1 STICK (¼ POUND) BUTTER OR
   MARGARINE, MELTED, PLUS
   SOME TO GREASE THE DISH

¼ CUP GOLDEN BROWN SUGAR,
   FIRMLY PACKED
1 TABLESPOON WATER
2 TABLESPOONS LEMON JUICE

MAKES 4 TO 6
SERVINGS

Preheat oven to 350°F. Thoroughly butter a medium baking dish.

Remove skins from boiled potatoes and quarter. Place in baking dish; pour butter over sweet potatoes; sprinkle with brown sugar. Combine water and lemon juice and add to potatoes. Brown in the oven until syrup is formed and potatoes have lightly browned and taken up the syrup, 15 to 20 minutes. Serve piping hot.

Uncle Henry Beecher grew a large field of sweet taters every year, let them cure a little bit, then shared them with family and friends. He thought they ought to be sweetened a bit!

Effie loved his full-fleshed, mature potatoes and thus made pies, biscuits, and puddings with them. She also baked them whole and unpeeled to serve with pork dishes.

A Golden Anniversary Cake

MAKES ONE 9-INCH, 3-LAYER CAKE

Women of my mother's generation loved to make tall three- and four-layer cakes. During the spring and summer months we celebrated festive occasions with white or silver cakes. But in the fall when the leaves were dropping, and our old people, married for fifty golden years, celebrated, nothing but a golden cake would do.

¾ CUP BUTTER (NO SUBSTITUTE)
1½ CUPS SUGAR
1 TEASPOON LEMON EXTRACT
8 EGG YOLKS, WELL BEATEN
3 CUPS CAKE FLOUR
3 TEASPOONS BAKING POWDER
½ TEASPOON SALT
1 CUP MILK
GOLDEN GLOW FROSTING (RECIPE FOLLOWS)

Preheat oven to 375°F. Thoroughly grease and flour three 9-inch layer cake pans.

In a large bowl cream the butter until smooth. Add sugar a little at a time, beating after each addition. Stir in the extract. Add egg yolks and continue beating. Into a medium bowl sift flour with baking powder and salt, and sift again. Alternately add the flour and the milk to the butter-sugar mixture, beating well after each addition. Turn batter into prepared cake pans.

Bake until cake is golden brown, pulls away from the pan when tipped, and springs back when touched, 20 minutes. Remove from oven and set pans on a wire rack. Layers should cool for 10 minutes in the pan before being turned out onto rack to cool completely. Fill and frost with Golden Glow Frosting.

Golden Glow Frosting

MAKES ENOUGH FOR ONE 9-INCH, 3-LAYER CAKE

½ CUP BUTTER SOFTENED AT ROOM TEMPERATURE
4½ CUPS POWDERED SUGAR
1 TEASPOON LEMON EXTRACT
2 TABLESPOONS GRATED ORANGE ZEST
3 TABLESPOONS STRAINED ORANGE JUICE, MORE IF NEEDED

In a medium bowl blend butter and sugar. Stir in lemon extract, orange zest, and orange juice; beat until frosting is smooth and of a spreading consistency.

BESIDE A HARVEST FIELD

I would not ask a holier place than this for prayer.
Here by this harvest field I stand, with my head bare,
And gaze through rows of corn shocks stretching on for miles,
Beholding in them majesty not found in cloistered aisles.
I scan the lengthy furrowed turf where plowmen's feet have trod,
And close beside their steps I see the footprints of my God.
My heart is rapt with inner joy that I can scarce contain
As from a distant field I hear the harvesters' refrain.
I cannot join their harvest song; my lips are sealed with awe
Lest I by faltering note should mar their praises of God's law;
Their praises of the truth concealed in grain that fell to earth
To lose itself and come again as something given birth,
To grow in blade and sturdy stem and then in ripened ear —
Who would not stand in silent awe and worship here?
I would not seek a holier place than this to pray;
I here forever would remain were that God's way.
But He who brought the harvest to this golden field
Has many garners to be filled with His rich yield.
I haste away, for human heart await the truth I've found
As I have here communed with Him on holy ground.

BERTHA M. RUSSELL
Best Loved Unity Poems

Here by the Harvest Field I Stand

M Y FAMILY RAISED ALL SORTS OF CORN——BEING MIDWESTERNERS THEY HAD A SPECIAL FONDNESS FOR IT. CORN FOR SUPPER TO THEM MEANT CORN AND BUTTER, FIVE OR SIX EARS, AND LITTLE ELSE. GRANDPA RAISED SWEET CORN, POPCORN, AND FIELD CORN FOR HOMINY, CORNMEAL, AND LIVESTOCK FEED. WHEN I WAS A CHILD, HE TOLD ME THAT HE THOUGHT POPCORN PLANTED TOO CLOSE TO HIS OTHER CORN WOULD CROSS-POLLINATE AND WOULD NOT POP; HE SHOWED ME HOW THE WIND WOULD BLOW THE POLLEN FROM THE LAST ROW OF CORN INTO ANOTHER ROW OF VEGETABLES UNLESS THE CORN WAS PLANTED IN BLOCKS TO ENSURE POLLINATION.

IT WAS FROM HIM I LEARNED THAT SWEET CORN CAN RANGE IN SIZE FROM FOUR-INCH EARS GROWN ON TWO-AND-A-HALF-FOOT STALKS TO SEVEN- OR EIGHT-INCH EARS GROWN ON EIGHT-FOOT STALKS. HE ALSO TOLD ME THAT CORN VARIES IN COLOR FROM YELLOW TO WHITE TO PURPLE, AND THAT THE COB MAY BE WHITE OR RED.

THE PLOW, SPADE, AND HOE

The farmer is chief of the nation,
The oldest of nobles is he;
How blest beyond others his station,
From want and from envy how free!
His patent was granted in Eden,
Long ages and ages ago;
O the farmer, the farmer forever,
Three cheers for the plow, spade, and hoe.

In April, when nature is waking,
And blue birds are first on the wing,
His plow now the fallows are breaking,
Whence beautiful harvest shall spring;
Then broadcast along the brown furrow,
We hasten the good seed to sow;
O the farmer, the farmer forever,
Three cheers for the plow, spade, and hoe.

But when, in the clear Autumn weather,
He reaps the reward of his care;
So busy and joyful together,
What monarch with him can compare?
His barns running over with plenty,
His trees with their fruit bending low;
O the farmer, the farmer forever,
Three cheers for the plow, spade, and hoe.

Then sing me the life of a farmer,
With comfort and health in his train,
And heed not the voice of the charmer,
That whispers of speedier gain;
With all the rich treasures 'tis teeming,
That heaven on man can bestow;
O the farmer, the farmer forever,
Three cheers for the plow, spade, and hoe.

ANONYMOUS
The Patron

THE RIPENED EAR

$\mathcal{B}$efore the Civil War, nine out of ten families were country people whose lives depended on agriculture. Many farms across the nation, but primarily those in the South, had been devastated during the War. The fields were ravaged, barns burned, horses, cattle, and other livestock driven off. Small landholders in the North and great plantation owners in the South had lost valuable manpower, which is always at the heart of agricultural prosperity.

Country folk were physically exhausted, financially impoverished, and emotionally unable to pull themselves up and make a new start. Then like a trickle before a flood, knowledge of an organization called the Grange and then the National Grange began to drift across the nation through the fields and into the homes.

Spirits began to lift; farm folk began to go see for themselves what the Grange, a developing farm organization, was about. They found their neighbors and friends packed in an old schoolhouse or in the back of a store. They found themselves bathed in an atmosphere that healed, taught, and encouraged. They learned about new methods of agriculture, better health care for children. Cooperation among families encouraged by the Grange helped to improve conditions. People united and neighbors became the officers of the Grange in their community. At the outset women were given the right to vote and held various offices.

Throughout the generations, the National Grange has continued to improve the life of its members and society in general. It was the Grange that brought electricity and rural delivery to the farms across the country. Many men and women today owe their college educations to Grange scholarships.

From Hither Come

As the shades of evening softly
Over town and country fall,
Brightly, thro' the gathering darkness,
Shines the lights from Patron's* hall,
And as we are wont to hasten
Fondly to our Father's home,
Guided by the evening lamplight,
Brothers, sisters, hither come.

Mrs. E. R. Smith/ W. B. Bradbury
The Patron

*Patron of husbandry

Maple Syrup Popcorn Balls

½ POUND POPCORN	2 TEASPOONS CREAM OF TARTAR	MAKES 24–26
⅔ CUP MAPLE SYRUP	2 TABLESPOONS MELTED BUTTER	POPCORN BALLS
2 CUPS SUGAR	⅛ TEASPOON BAKING SODA	DEPENDING ON SIZE
⅔ CUP BOILING WATER	1 TABLESPOON MAPLE FLAVORING	
2 TABLESPOONS VINEGAR		

In a large pan pop all of the corn. Turn it into a large bowl or pan. In a large saucepan combine syrup, sugar, water, and vinegar. Heat to boiling. Add cream of tartar. Boil to a soft crack stage (275° to 280°F). Remove from heat; add butter, baking soda, and maple flavoring. Stir gently. Pour over popcorn. Cool only until popcorn can be hand-shaped into balls.

As Indian summer faded, it became too cold for my sister and me to play outside, so Mama played table games with us indoors. Then, late in the afternoon, just before our father and grandfather were expected for supper, she made maple syrup popcorn balls for an evening treat.

SUNDAY COMPANY

THE MAPLE TREE

The old maple tree
still hovers
'round the long rope swing
where once children sat
feet first
tickling the sky.

<small>PATRICIA PARISH KUHN</small>

*W*hen Mother was young, the Meekins family, Grandpa, Grandma, Grandpa's sisters and brother, their wives and children, all went to church on Sunday morning. Grandpa and his sons, like other men in the community, brought their guitars, mandolins, fiddles, and banjos with them and often played along with the choir.

Mother particularly loved to hear the old hymns: "Abide with Me," "He Keeps Me Singing," "By His Stripes We Are Healed," "Love Lifted Me," "Dwelling in Beulah Land," "The Old Rugged Cross," and "The Last Mile of the Way."

When the service was over, the family of fifteen to twenty-four strong flowed up the aisle and shook hands with the preacher. Then the elder members gathered up the small children, and they all climbed into the lumber wagons and settled down in a nest of clean, worn feather mattresses and comforters. In no time, the two or three wagons were rolling down the dirt road toward home. The folks were still filled with "joy unspeakable," so they sang every hymn they had ever known, in harmony. Men's voices poured through the valleys. Women sang, their light and delicate voices sounding like angels on the wing.

At home lay the makings of a great Sunday dinner. By one or two o'clock the women and girls had the tables set with seats enough for all of the family and friends who had been invited outside the church, as well as neighborhood teenage farm boys who would show up. This latter group, though young, knew that the Meekins girls and women were exceptionally good cooks and that they would bake fancy pies and cakes, especially for Sunday dinner.

Roast Pheasant or Grouse

2 BIRDS

MELTED BUTTER AS NEEDED FOR

   COATING BIRDS

SALT AND PEPPER AS DESIRED

1 TABLESPOON CHERVIL

½ TEASPOON MARJORAM

4 TO 6 SLICES FARM-STYLE BACON

MAKES 4 SERVINGS

Every fall neighbors come by with a pheasant or two. While nothing is ever said, except thank you, we know that their gift is a show of appreciation for a bit of tractor work or a little smoking of mountain trout that Raymond has done for them without charge throughout the year.

Preheat oven to 300°F. Wipe the birds clean and rub them with butter, salt, and pepper. Rub chervil and marjoram between your fingers and sprinkle them over the birds. Place seasoned birds in a close-fitting pan and cover with bacon. Insert a meat thermometer into the breast and bake until it reads 180°F. If you suspect the bird to be an older one, add ¼ cup water, cover the pan, and cook until it appears tender and done.

Colleen's Fancy Coconut Carrot Salad

1⅓ CUPS SWEET FLAKED COCONUT

1½ CUPS FINELY SHREDDED

   CARROTS

½ CUP SLIVERED ALMONDS

¼ CUP GOLDEN RAISINS

½ CUP MAYONNAISE

2 TABLESPOONS LEMON JUICE

½ TEASPOON GROUND GINGER

MAKES 6 OR MORE SERVINGS

After the first heavy frost in October and on into the colder months, women in our family begin to create new salads to replace summer greens, tomatoes, and all of the other delicious vegetables of fall.

In a medium bowl combine coconut, carrots, almonds, and raisins. In a small bowl combine mayonnaise, lemon juice, and ginger. Pour dressing over coconut-raisin mixture. Stir to blend. Refrigerate just long enough to chill. Serve immediately with baked ham.

Country Style Potatoes

MAKES 6 SERVINGS

Since all of Grandpa's children grew up on red potatoes, they tend to fry, bake, scallop, and prepare them in numerous other ways as well. This is one of their tasty creations.

1 TABLESPOON MINCED ONION

3 TABLESPOONS MARGARINE

3 CUPS RED POTATOES, BOILED, PEELED, AND DICED

SALT AND PEPPER AS DESIRED

1 TABLESPOON MINCED PARSLEY

In a large frying pan brown the onion in margarine. Add prepared potatoes; salt and pepper to taste. Turn heat down and cook onion-potato mixture slowly, stirring frequently until brown. Serve hot, garnished with parsley.

Sweet Potato Pecan Custard

MAKES 1 QUART

Uncle Henry Beecher grew great fields of "sweet taters," which he sold and gave away to friends and neighbors along with his clover honey. He also kept some for himself and used them in this recipe.

2 CUPS SWEET POTATOES, COOKED, MASHED, AND SIEVED

¾ TEASPOON CINNAMON

½ TEASPOON NUTMEG

¼ TEASPOON GINGER

3 EGGS, BEATEN TO A FROTH

1½ CUPS THIN CREAM (HALF AND HALF WILL DO NICELY)

A FEW GRAINS OF SALT

⅓ TO ½ CUP STRAINED HONEY

1 CUP PECANS, CHOPPED

Preheat oven to 425°F. Set out and lightly grease a 1-quart round baking dish.

In a medium bowl combine sweet potato pulp, spices, eggs, cream, and salt. Pour into prepared baking dish. Bake until a dinner-knife blade inserted into the center of the custard comes out clean, 25 minutes. When done, remove from oven and set out on a wire rack to cool. Just before serving cover top of custard with honey and chopped pecans.

HARVEST FESTIVALS

When the last warmth of Indian Summer has faded away,
and bleak fall winds drive scudding grey
clouds across the sky, Fall is on the wane.
Barns are made snug.

Late harvested apples, nuts
and vegetables are securely tucked
into boxes, baskets and bins; cellars,
storerooms, and pantries are full.
Winter is secure.

Safe from wind and weather,
homefolk settled down before a roaring
fire, rest after the season's labor,
and rejoice over the earth's bountiful gifts.
Nature's circle has come full around.

JANE WATSON HOPPING

ABOUT A BOUNTEOUS HARVEST SHARED

The first summer that our daughter, Colleen, and Mark were married, we planted both upper and lower gardens, each about 250 by 75 feet in size. Mark worked tirelessly at planting and hoeing. We all helped, putting in many varieties of plants and seeds. There were three or four kinds of tomatoes, some for early salads, others for winter sauces, in all shades of yellow, orange, pink, and red. There were long rows of potatoes, green and yellow snap beans, red and yellow onions, banana, bell, and hot peppers, Golden Acre, red, and savoy cabbages, which grew abundantly in the fertile soil on the upper side of the creek.

In the lower garden were great patches of winter squash, corn, cucumbers, and pumpkins of every ilk covering the well-tilled earth. Along one side stood an eight-foot-high row of sorghum cane, the stalks of which we would run through the mill to release the juice and then cook down into sorghum molasses.

All through the growing season we took turns weeding and picking, canning, freezing, and drying vegetables. Then in September, we quit watering so that tomatoes and peppers would firm up, and squashes, pumpkins, and melons would mature. Finally, in early October before the first frost, we picked everything that was left in the garden. This included all of the great squashes—some of the banana squashes were 48 inches long and were so heavy I couldn't lift them. There were also endless rows of tomatoes, cabbages, and more. The potatoes, already dug, had been washed and put in storage. The onions we had pulled and aged were piled in baskets.

Eventually all was gathered in and piled in boxes and baskets all over the back lawn. We stood about and admired the results of our labor. Each family decided what more they needed to feed them through the winter. Then, together, we chose this and that to share with friends and neighbors. And, finally, after much deliberation, we decided how much we would give to various charitable organizations: the Gospel Mission, Salvation Army, Access, Loaves and Fishes. We took boxes of vegetables to the Grange hall to share there, and hauled a truckload more into town.

As I saw the pleasure on Mark's and Colleen's faces, I thought: In each person's life there should come, at least once, a time of plenty, a remembered, almost religious experience of Mother Earth's bounty, and the promise of an abundant life.

Turkey Vegetable Soup with Homemade Croutons

1 SMALL ONION, CHOPPED

2 TABLESPOONS BUTTER OR
    MARGARINE

2 CUPS WATER

1 CUP LEFTOVER TURKEY GRAVY

2 CUPS TURKEY, DICED

½ CUP CELERY TOPS AND PIECES

1½ CUPS DICED POTATOES

1 CUP DICED CARROTS

2½ CUPS MILK

2 TABLESPOONS FLOUR

1 TEASPOON SALT, OR TO TASTE

⅛ TEASPOON BLACK PEPPER

HOMEMADE CROUTONS (RECIPE
    FOLLOWS)

MAKES 6 OR MORE
SERVINGS

This easy-to-make leftover turkey soup has always been an after-Thanksgiving treat. When served with homemade croutons or simple bread, it pleases everyone.

In the Dutch oven sauté onion and butter or margarine until tender but not browned. Add water, gravy, turkey, and vegetables. Stir over medium heat to blend. Boil gently, covered, until vegetables are tender. Stir a small amount of the milk into the flour. When smooth, stir in remaining milk, salt, and pepper. Add milk mixture to the hot soup. Simmer. Stir occasionally to prevent sticking until soup is slightly thickened. Serve in large, deep soup bowls with Homemade Croutons or a simple bread.

Homemade Croutons

6 SLICES BREAD

4 TABLESPOONS BUTTER OR
    MARGARINE, SOFTENED AT
    ROOM TEMPERATURE

¼ TEASPOON GARLIC SALT OR A
    SMALL AMOUNT OF PUREED
    GARLIC

PAPRIKA

MAKES 6 SERVINGS

Preheat oven to 300°F. Set out a medium baking sheet.

Trim crusts of bread. Blend butter or margarine with garlic salt or puree. Spread on both sides of bread. Cut slices of bread into cubes; place them on baking sheet and sprinkle with paprika.

Bake until crisp and golden brown, 20 to 30 minutes. Serve piping hot with soup.

From UNFRAMED PICTURES

A cluster of trees by the creek
Just as the sun goes down —
Their branches etched
Against the flaming sky.

GRACE E. HALL
Patchwork

Sunlit and Warm with Indian Summer

EARLY IN OCTOBER, BEFORE COLD NIGHTS DIP BELOW THIRTY DEGREES, FARMERS AND GARDENERS MUST DRIVE THEMSELVES TO BRING IN THE HARVEST BEFORE THE FIRST FROST KILLS OFF TENDER CROPS LIKE SNAP BEANS, TOMATOES, PEPPERS, AND WATERMELONS. FOLLOWING THE FROST COME MANY DAYS OF WARM, HAZY SUNSHINE. THERE IS A BITE IN THE AIR, A FRESHNESS THAT INSPIRES PEOPLE TO WRITE AND SING THE PRAISES OF OCTOBER AND INDIAN SUMMER.

LEAVES CHANGE COLOR FROM THEIR GREEN SUMMER DRESS TO GOLD, RUSSET, AND BRILLIANT CRIMSON. IN THE FIELDS BLOOM GOLDENROD, FRINGED GENTIAN, AND WILD ASTERS. MANY BIRDS FLY SOUTH, LEAVING BEHIND SEED EATERS LIKE SPARROWS THAT FEAST IN DRY FIELDS AND MEADOWS.

AROUND HALLOWEEN, THE COLD RETURNS, AND PICKERS HARVEST LATE FRUITS LIKE PERSIMMON, APPLES, AND COLD-RESISTANT GRAPES.

OLD BLUE OCTOBER

In late fall, when outside temperatures began to drop, Mother, Ada, and sometimes Effie went to call on Old Missus Upjohn. They always took a few little sweets to go with her many-flavored teas. Mother recalls sampling her ginger tea, which had a nice warm, spicy flavor and was sweetened with golden brown sugar.

Just as they were leaving, Missus Upjohn shared one of her blends with them: orange peel and lemon peel pulverized with honey and ¼ teaspoon of strong ginger, pulverized or ground, steeped in a pint or more of boiling water.

CHAMOMILE TEAS

*O*ld Missus Upjohn swears that chamomile tea, made from flowers, has always been a healthful after-dinner drink. For making teas, she uses one part chamomile and one part peppermint or one of the other mint flavors, such as apple mint or pineapple mint. To top off the evening, she favors chamomile tea made with lemon verbena and lavender. One of her healthful blends before dinner is chamomile tea with grated fresh ginger. If you prefer it after you have eaten, she recommends serving it with fennel, sweetened with honey and finished off with lemon or orange slices.

Ada's Oatmeal Icebox Cookies

1 CUP BUTTER OR MARGARINE

1 CUP LIGHT BROWN SUGAR

⅔ CUP GRANULATED SUGAR

2 EGGS, WELL BEATEN

1 TEASPOON VANILLA EXTRACT

1½ CUPS ALL-PURPOSE FLOUR

1½ TEASPOONS BAKING SODA

⅛ TEASPOON SALT

3 CUPS QUICK-COOKING OATS

1 CUP FINELY CHOPPED WALNUTS

 (OPTIONAL)

MAKES 4 DOZEN

OR MORE

Since many families come early to the reunion and Thanksgiving festivities, which often last for nearly a week, women who come from afar bring baskets and tins of cookies for snacks, coffee breaks, hungry, fussy children, and loved old folks.

In a large bowl, cream the butter until light, add brown and granulated sugar gradually, and continue creaming until well blended. Add eggs and vanilla; stir until incorporated. Add flour, sifted once with baking soda and salt. Stir to make a batter, then fold in the oats and the walnuts if desired. Divide the dough in half, shape each half into rough logs, wrap in waxed paper, and chill. About 15 to 20 minutes before cookies are ready to bake, preheat oven to 375°F. Set out a large cookie sheet.

Take half of the dough out of the refrigerator. Slice and bake for 12 to 14 minutes. Remove from oven and transfer to a brown paper or wire rack. Repeat with second half of the dough. When cookies are thoroughly cooled, store them in an airtight container.

From Time of Clearer Twitterings

Season halest of the year!
How the zestful atmosphere
Nettles blood and brain and smites
Into life the old delights
We have wasted in our youth,
And our graver years, forsooth!
How again the boyish heart
Leaps to see the chipmunk start
From the brush and sleek the sun's
Very beauty, as he runs!
How again a subtle hint
Of crushed pennyroyal or mint
Sends us on our knees, as when
We were truant boys of ten —
Brown marauders of the wood,
Merrier than Robin Hood!

JAMES WHITCOMB RILEY
The Complete Works of James Whitcomb Riley

LEAVES IN RED AND GOLD
CHANGING COLOR OVERHEAD

*B*y mid-October, Indian summer is almost over. Days are colder, nights get nippy—frost is coming on. In the woods, leaves change from green to red, brown, yellow, and soft gray. With every breeze, trees lose their foliage, and stems loosen on oaks and elms.

Over woods and meadows mellow hazes gather. Hickory nuts, walnuts, butternuts, and pawpaws rattle down and drop on a richly colored bed of damp leaves. Overhead the honking of geese sailing south causes people to stop, look up, and perhaps imagine the warmer climes where the birds will settle for the winter.

North winds sweep the last roses of summer off their stems and scatter petals on breezes. The harvest, too, is grinding down. Only November clings to autumn as winter prepares to enter with December.

Easy-to-Make Curried Split Pea Soup

2 TABLESPOONS BUTTER OR
    MARGARINE, SOFTENED AT
    ROOM TEMPERATURE
1 TABLESPOON FLOUR
2½ CUPS CHICKEN BROTH, PLUS
    1 CHICKEN BOUILLON CUBE

1 CUP MILK
1½ CUPS COOKED SPLIT PEAS
1 TEASPOON CURRY POWDER

MAKES 6 TO 8
SERVINGS

In a ricer, colander, or blender, puree all ingredients and blend until smooth. Stir constantly while simmering over medium to low heat until thick.

Take saucepan off heat and transfer soup to a tureen.

Effie learned to make this delicious soup from women in her quilting circle. As always, she shared it with other women in the family, all of whom thought it was a great new soup to add to midwinter menus. As the months turned from December to March, women in each household tested this bread and that until they had just the right one to go with this soup. Many found that Whole Wheat Buttermilk Rolls (page 141) were a fine choice.

The End of Day

I come into the cool house at the end of day,
in from the dew and afternoon sun
My arms are bare and brown beneath rolled
*   sleeves*
of the soft blue work shirt you made,
faded now with years of washing.

I come into the cool house and I sit beside
the round table with the oilcloth cover,
in the light of the bright butterfly
that spreads evening wings in the globe,
and the lighter smell of kerosene.

Around the table we gather, at the end of day;
father, mother, sons and daughters, you
*   and I,*
We talk softly and share with each other
the stories of our day, the journey
that led us from the fields of home;
talk of our work in the fields, of home.
We talk softly of our day.
We join hands. We pray.
Evening closes gently around the lamplight,
finding us all together, a family, together.

ALVIN REISS

Wheat amid the Chaff

ALL THROUGH THE DEPRESSION OF THE THIRTIES AND THROUGH THE TRIALS OF WORLD WAR II, SHEILA AND I GREW UP IN THE EMBRACE OF OUR STRONG CLANNISH FAMILY. WE WERE TAUGHT BY THEM ALL TO MAKE DO; TO DO WHATEVER HAS TO BE DONE AND TO DO IT WELL. THEY WERE STERN WHEN WE COMPLAINED ABOUT EVERY LITTLE INCONVENIENCE OR MINOR TRAGEDY. THEY TOLD US TO LOOK FOR THE WHEAT AMID THE CHAFF IN LIFE. OFTEN WE WERE ADMONISHED AND TOLD TO KEEP IN MIND THAT EVERY DAY IS A DAY OF THANKSGIVING. MOTHER USED TO TELL US THAT GOD SENDS SHOWERS OF BLESSINGS TO THE DESERVING AND THE UNDESERVING ALIKE AND CALLS ON EACH ONE OF US TO BE MERCIFUL AND COMPASSIONATE TO THOSE AROUND US.

AND, JUST SO WE WOULD UNDERSTAND, SHE WOULD LAY BEFORE US BITS FOR PONDERING LIKE THIS ONE:

From BLESSED QUIETNESS

Blessed quietness, holy quietness,
What assurance in my soul;
On the stormy sea,
Speaking peace to me,
How the billows cease to roll.

M. P. FERGUSON
ARR. FROM W. S. MARSHALL
Songs of Praise

From A Sudden Shower

And then, abrupt — the rain! the rain! —
The earth lies gasping; and the eyes
Behind the streaming window-pane
Smile at the trouble of the skies.

JAMES WHITCOMB RILEY

THE DEW AND THE AFTERNOON SUN

Grandpa used to tell us stories about the years he lived in Black Lick, Ohio. When he was a little tad he had loved to wade through tender grass that glistened with dew. He and his older sisters would lie awake and listen to night birds outside their window calling softly in the twilight.

From childhood on he loved the farm, the harvest of autumn's treasures, the trees that flamed on a wooded hillside. He fondly remembered his parents going about their evening work, and the children as well all had chores, even the littlest ones.

When chores were done, he and his many brothers and sisters would sit on the porch and tell tall tales or sing songs. Sometimes their mother would sing the songs of her childhood in Maryland and Pennsylvania. If they begged her to, she would laugh and sing songs to them that had been brought across the water from Germany, her parents' native land.

GRANDMA'S LESSONS

The noisy Jays at the window box
always seemed to know,
The moment of the peanut harvest
in the garden just below.

When children gathered round about
as quick as quick could be
To watch those greedy wingèd ones
in total disharmony.

They'd fight and push and peck each other
in ways we never could,
Until grandmother's crooked cane
crashed hard upon the wood.

But grandma never missed a chance
to gently scold then teach,
That young'uns must never ever take
what's not within their reach.

PATRICIA PARISH KUHN

Apple Cider Yam Bread

MAKES 3 LOAVES

This quick sweet bread made with richly colored, orange-fleshed yams tastes almost like cake. Mother made it in late fall when the weather began to cool and the yams were big enough to dig.

4 CUPS ALL-PURPOSE FLOUR

1 TABLESPOON BAKING POWDER

2 TEASPOONS BAKING SODA

1½ TEASPOONS SALT

2 TEASPOONS GROUND CINNAMON

1 TEASPOON FRESHLY GRATED NUTMEG

½ TEASPOON GROUND CLOVES

1 CUP BUTTER OR MARGARINE, SOFTENED AT ROOM TEMPERATURE

1 POUND BOX (2⅓ CUPS) LIGHT BROWN SUGAR

2 CUPS ORANGE-FLESHED PRECOOKED YAMS, PUREED OR THOROUGHLY MASHED

1 CUP APPLE CIDER

4 EGGS, BEATEN TO A FROTH

1½ CUPS CHOPPED WALNUTS

2 CUPS DARK RAISINS

Preheat oven to 350°F. Grease three 9x5x3-inch loaf pans; set aside until needed.

Into a large bowl sift together flour, baking powder, baking soda, salt, cinnamon, nutmeg, and cloves; set aside. In a second large bowl, cream butter and brown sugar together until light and well blended. Add pureed yams, cider, and eggs. Stir until smooth and thoroughly blended. About *1 cup* at a time, add the flour mixture to the yam mixture, stirring well after each addition. *Don't beat this batter.* Fold in nuts and raisins. Spoon into prepared pans.

Bake until medium golden brown on top, about 45 minutes to 1 hour. Check doneness with a toothpick: Insert into the center of one loaf; if it comes out clean the loaves are done. Remove loaves from oven and let stand about 10 minutes, then turn onto a wire rack to cool. Serve warm or cold.

GLEANING THE FIELDS

*L*ate in October, when the crops were for the most part sold or stored away, the women often invited family members and hired workers who had helped with the harvest to share in a harvest breakfast.

Since the days were cold and rain threatened, breakfast was served at nine o'clock instead of five-thirty. The long trestle table was ladened with platters of ham and bowls of gravy, golden piles of scrambled eggs, piping hot biscuits and a basket full of Ada's graham nut muffins. Old-fashioned dishes held fresh butter and a variety of summer jams, jellies, and preserves. Children were served cold milk, while adults enjoyed steaming coffee.

When the day warmed up, all went into the fields to gather all sorts of vegetables that had been passed over during the main harvest and to stack them along the edge of the field. After this, they all were invited to take whatever they wished home with them.

Pork Tenderloin with Sweet Potatoes and Scrambled Eggs

2 TO 3 POUNDS PORK TENDERLOIN

1 OR MORE TEASPOONS SALT AS
    DESIRED

⅛ TO ¼ TEASPOON PEPPER AS
    DESIRED

6 MEDIUM SWEET POTATOES

SCRAMBLED EGGS (RECIPE
    FOLLOWS)

MAKES 6 TO 8
SERVINGS

This pork dish was often served late in the morning after farm folk had already been out in the fields for several hours. Today we might call a meal like this a brunch.

Wipe tenderloins, place in an open roasting pan, and brown quickly in a hot (425°F) oven. Sprinkle with salt and pepper and continue to bake meat at 375°F for 45 minutes or until internal temperature reaches 160°F on a meat thermometer; baste every 15 minutes.

Pare and parboil the sweet potatoes, allowing 10 minutes cooking time. Drain and arrange potatoes in pan around meat. Cook until potatoes are soft, basting every 10 minutes along with the meat.

When meat and potatoes are almost done, scramble the eggs. Serve tenderloins, sweet potatoes, and eggs at the same time, while still hot.

Scrambled Eggs

MAKES 6 TO 8 SERVINGS	5 EGGS, LIGHTLY BEATEN	½ CUP MILK
	½ TEASPOON SALT	2 TABLESPOONS BUTTER
	⅛ TEASPOON PEPPER	

To beaten eggs add salt, pepper, and milk; stir to blend. Melt butter in heated omelet or frying pan; pour butter into egg mixture; stir together. Turn egg mixture into frying pan. Cook over medium-low heat, stirring and scraping the bottom of the pan constantly, until eggs are creamy and done. Serve immediately.

A GIFT OF BURNISHED RIBBONS

SPENDING A DAY

Splendid things may happen!
Oh, of course they may;
But thinking of tomorrow
Is no way to spend today!

MARY CAROLYN DAVIES
Best Loved Unity Poems

*W*hen Mary Ann, Ada's granddaughter, was five years old, her father was far away in Texas, helping his father take care of his mother, who was quite old and ill. Mary Ann's older brother, Howard, who was up north in college, was going to spend Thanksgiving with his new girlfriend and her family. That left only her mother, Bert, her younger brother, and herself at home for the holiday. Bert (age 10) spent all of his time at the school playing touch football with other boys.

Much to Bert's disgust, Mary Ann spent long hours in the playhouse their father had built for her before he went away, and too often she cried herself to sleep. Her mother, a loving, kind woman, tried to comfort her. She promised Mary Ann and Bert that she would take them to their other grandma's house for Thanksgiving dinner and that they would stay the night.

When the day arrived, Mary Ann woke up early. She bounded out of bed, washed her face and hands, had her breakfast, put on clean underwear and stockings, slipped into her new apple-green party dress and shining black shoes. Then she ran downstairs to show her mother but, upon getting there, she remembered that she had forgotten a ribbon for her hair. So she ran back upstairs to her bedroom, opened the door, and saw on her bed a pile of ribbons of all colors: rust, gold, bronze, yellow, cream, dark pine

y a crookedly folded piece of paper. She opened it and saw
ribbon in her hair and a boy, not much taller, with a wide
e was only five years old, she knew that the writing said:

ᴐ German Pancake with Apple Topping

3 LARGE EGGS, BEATEN UNTIL
  FOAMY
¾ CUP MILK
¾ CUP ALL-PURPOSE FLOUR
½ TEASPOON SALT
6 TABLESPOONS BUTTER OR
  MARGARINE

3 CUPS TART APPLES (STAYMANS
  PREFERRED), PEELED, CORED,
  AND THINLY SLICED
¼ CUP GRANULATED SUGAR
1 TEASPOON GROUND CINNAMON
3 TABLESPOONS POWDERED SUGAR

MAKES 6 SERVINGS

When Mother was growing up, she learned from her German women neighbors how to make many delicious dishes, among them this oven-baked pancake dish. Through the years it has become a favorite family treat on cold fall mornings.

Preheat oven to 450°F.

In a large bowl combine eggs and milk. Add flour and salt; stir just until dry ingredients are moistened. Over medium heat in a heavy 12-inch cast-iron or ovenproof skillet, melt 2 tablespoons butter. Pour batter into skillet and bake in oven 15 minutes. After 5 to 7 minutes, check pancake and prick any large bubbles with a fork. When the 15 minutes are up, lower oven temperature to 350°F. Bake until pancake is crisp and lightly browned, an additional 10 minutes.

While pancake is baking, prepare topping. In a medium skillet over medium heat, melt the remaining 4 tablespoons butter. Add apples, granulated sugar, and cinnamon. Sauté mixture until apples are tender, 10 to 15 minutes.

When pancake is done, slide it out of the pan onto a platter. Spoon apple mixture over the top. Sprinkle with powdered sugar. Cut into wedges and serve while piping hot.

Note: Stayman apples are available October through March. This juicy, slightly tart, red-striped apple is excellent for toppings like the above as well as for pies and baking. Rhode Island Greening, Rome Beauty, or Spitzenberg may also be used in this dish.

FROSTED WINDOWPANES AND WARM FIRES

From JACK FROST

Oh, Jack Frost plays so many, many tricks,
He is so very pert and bold
He pinches the cheeks,
And he tweaks the nose
And he turns us blue with cold, cold, cold,
And he turns us blue with cold.

ALICE C. D. RILEY

*O*n chill autumn days, Grandpa bundled us up and took us outside with him to see the wonders a cold night could bring: fences dressed in lace, broken water pipe sculptures, late garden vegetables coated with a filigree of ice, frosted flakes on the window.

When our fingers were icy and our clothes wet, he would hug us a bit to warm us up and then send us inside to wait by the fire. Soon he would come in, his arms stacked with cord wood. He would tell Mother, "These children need something hot to drink," and in no time at all we would be sipping hot milk or hot chocolate.

Aunt El's Sweet Milk Doughnuts

MAKES 3 TO 4 DOZEN

Huge batches of these doughnuts were made when our old families gathered at Aunt El's to visit, share with each other family gossip, and

2 EGGS, BEATEN TO A FROTH
1 CUP SUGAR
4¾ CUPS ALL-PURPOSE FLOUR
1 TABLESPOON BAKING POWDER
1 TEASPOON SALT
½ TEASPOON CINNAMON
½ TEASPOON NUTMEG
⅛ TEASPOON GINGER
1 CUP MILK

2 TABLESPOONS MELTED BUTTER
    OR MARGARINE
½ TEASPOON VANILLA EXTRACT
½ TEASPOON LEMON EXTRACT
COOKING OIL FOR DEEP-FAT FRYING
GRANULATED OR POWDERED
    SUGAR AS NEEDED FOR
    SPRINKLING OVER OR
    DUSTING COOKED DOUGHNUTS

In a large bowl blend eggs and sugar together. Into a second large bowl sift flour with baking powder, salt, and spices. Alternately add to egg-sugar mixture with combined milk, melted butter, vanilla, and lemon extract. Chill dough.

Meanwhile, preheat cooking oil to 365°F. Remove chilled dough from refrigerator. Turn out onto lightly floured surface. Roll out dough to ½-inch thickness. Cut with floured cutter. Deep fry until brown on both sides. Drain on crumpled absorbent paper (heavy-duty paper towels will do nicely). Sprinkle both sides with granulated or powdered sugar as desired.

exchange recipes and hometown news.

*C*veryone—great-grandparents, Mother's sisters and brothers, on down through the generations to cousins who were not even eight years old—sat down to a cold luncheon. Women and girls set out platters of cold meat and salads, fresh bread, coffee, tea, and icy cold milk and sweet cider, which was passed around until everyone was fed.

Young girls cleared the table and washed the dishes while women, young and old, eagerly set about the annual cookoff. Soon doughnuts by the hundreds were ready to eat. Some years they baked four or five batches at a time, some for family and neighbors who dropped in, others to pack into gift baskets and brightly colored calico bags.

Older children who knew their way about the city then would deliver hot doughnuts to old folks and those whose health was failin'.

An Old-Time Milk Punch

| 2 TABLESPOONS SUGAR | 1 CUP MILK | MAKES 1 TALL |
| ½ TEASPOON VANILLA | ¼ CUP SPARKLING WATER | GLASSFUL OF PUNCH |

In a small bowl combine sugar, vanilla, and milk. Stir well, then add sparkling water. Pour punch from one small bowl to another to make it froth (hold the bowl high as you pour the liquid back and forth). When it's frothy, pour into a tall glass and serve.

Children and adults in our extended family have through the years thought this drink was a perfect complement to slightly warm doughnuts.

Wind in the Trees

MOTHER HAS ALWAYS LOVED FALL WEATHER, PARTICULARLY THE FEW CLEAR DAYS WHEN DADDY WAS AT WORK AND SHEILA AND I WERE AT SCHOOL. ON SUCH DAYS SHE WOULD GET HER WORK DONE AND SPEND SOME TIME OUT OF DOORS DIGGING IN HER FLOWER BEDS, PICKING HUGE BOUQUETS OFF HER LINGERING LAVENDER CHRYSANTHEMUMS.

IF THE DAY TURNED COLD, SHE WOULD BUNDLE UP IN HER FARM COAT AND PUT ON HER OLD STRAW HAT, DADDY'S WARM STOCKINGS, AND HER OWN KNEE-HIGH RUBBER BOOTS. AND OFF SHE'D GO WITH HER WHEELBARROW AROUND BEHIND THE BARN TO SCRAPE UP LEAF MOLD FOR HER FLOWER BEDS. IF THE WEATHER HELD, SHE WOULD SNIP A LITTLE DEADWOOD OFF HER ROSES.

IF SHE GOT TIRED, SHE WOULD FIND A SPOT IN HER WINTER GARDEN, A PLACE TO SIT AND GAZE AT SLICK, DARKLY THREATENING RAIN CLOUDS. WHEN THE SOUND OF WIND CHIMES ON BOTH FRONT AND BACK PORCHES BEGAN TO SING, SHE WOULD GET UP AND WALK THROUGH THE YARD TO WATCH THE TREES SWAY AND THE FLOCKS OF BIRDS THAT HAD SETTLED IN THE PASTURE, FEASTING ON SEEDS AND WORMS.

From BROAD AS THE SKY

God speaks to me in the stir of a leaf,
In the glorious song of a bird;
And my pew is a log or a mountain crag —
Wherever His voice is heard.

G. C. CONSTABLE
Best Loved Unity Poems

EVER THANKFUL

On Thanksgiving morning, our family and friends gathered quite early to share breakfast before the festivities began. Usually that meant six to twelve people at the table. Effie often brought link sausages with apple rings; Ada's favorite fancy holiday dish was creamed dried beef and eggs in toast cups. Aunt Irene, Aunt Mabel, and others brought coffee cakes, sweet breads, and cookies enough for snacking throughout the day and evening.

From SUFFICIENCY

There is sufficient for this day
Of every good the heart can hold,
And with tomorrow's dawning light
Tomorrow's blessings shall unfold.

R. H. GRENVILLE
Best Loved Unity Poems

Effie's Link Sausages with Apple Rings

MAKES 4 TO 6 SERVINGS

Breakfast at Effie's house was a momentous occasion. She fried platters of link sausages and apple rings. Mother and other girls scurried off to the springhouse for icy cold milk, coffee cream, homemade butter, and soft homemade cheese. Out of the pie safe came hot loaves of bread.

Men and boys gathered around the table, eager to say Grace and eat.

1 POUND SAUSAGE (16 LINKS)
4 MEDIUM APPLES (WINESAP PREFERRED)
3 TABLESPOONS RESERVED SAUSAGE DRIPPINGS

⅓ CUP FIRMLY PACKED GOLDEN BROWN SUGAR
½ TEASPOON FRESHLY GRATED NUTMEG (GROUND MAY BE USED)

Place sausage links in a large cold skillet; add 2 tablespoons cold water. (If skillet will not hold all the sausages, cook half at a time.) Cover and cook over medium heat for 8 to 10 minutes. Remove cover and drain off liquid; brown links and turn as necessary (do not prick links with a fork). As drippings collect, pour them into a heatproof bowl; reserve 3 tablespoons sausage drippings.

Wash and core apples. Cut each into about 5 slices ½ to ¼ inch thick. When sausage links are browned, remove from pan. Drain on absorbent paper. Set aside while cooking apple slices.

Place apple slices flat in hot skillet with reserved drippings. Cook over low heat until apple rings are tender-crisp. Stir together brown sugar and nutmeg. Sprinkle over apple rings. Continue cooking gently until sugar is completely melted. Serve immediately with sausage links.

Ada's Dried Beef Toast Cups

MAKES 6 SERVINGS

To save time, one of her daughters helped Ada prepare the toast cups, another would prepare the hard-

4 HARD-COOKED EGGS (INSTRUCTIONS FOLLOW)
6 TOAST CUPS (INSTRUCTIONS FOLLOW)
2 CUPS MEDIUM WHITE SAUCE (RECIPE FOLLOWS)

⅓ CUP (ABOUT 3¼ OUNCES) SLICED AND SAUTÉED OR CANNED, DRAINED MUSHROOMS
1 CUP (ABOUT 2½ OUNCES) SHREDDED OR MINCED DRIED BEEF
¼ CUP MINCED PARSLEY

Prepare Hard-Cooked Eggs and Toast Cups and set aside. Meanwhile, make Medium White Sauce and keep hot. Force egg yolks through a sieve or ricer and set aside for a garnish. Chop egg whites and set aside. Begin browning the Toast Cups. Add mushrooms, egg whites, and shredded dried beef to pan of white sauce and stir. Cook mixture, stirring occasionally, bringing to serving temperature, about 1 or 2 minutes. Spoon into toast cups. Sprinkle sieved egg yolks over Toast Cups, garnish with minced parsley, and serve immediately.

cooked eggs, another the medium-white sauce, and her youngest daughter would slice and mince mushrooms, dried beef, and parsley. With all the parts ready, Ada could then quickly assemble her festive dish for a family holiday breakfast.

Hard-Cooked Eggs

Cover eggs with water and bring to a boil. Turn off heat and let eggs stand covered 20 to 22 minutes. Then plunge them into running cold water. For easy shelling, immediately crack shells under the water and roll eggs between hands to loosen shell. When eggs are cool, start peeling them at the large end.

Toast Cups

6 SLICES BREAD **¼ CUP MELTED BUTTER OR MARGARINE** **MAKES 6 TOAST CUPS**

At our house, Mother, who was organized and a good cook, liked to prepare the toast cups all by herself.

Remove crusts from bread. Lightly brush both sides of slices with melted butter or margarine. Gently press each slice into a muffin cup to form a shell. Just before filling toast cups, lightly brown them in the oven, 5 to 8 minutes.

Medium White Sauce

MAKES ABOUT 1 CUP
SAUCE

2 TABLESPOONS BUTTER OR
MARGARINE
2 TABLESPOONS ALL-PURPOSE
FLOUR

¼ TEASPOON SALT
A FEW GRAINS BLACK PEPPER
1 CUP MILK

Melt butter in a saucepan over low heat. Blend in flour, salt, and pepper. Heat until mixture bubbles. Remove from heat and gradually stir in the milk. Cook until sauce thickens, 1 to 2 minutes longer.

Ada's Graham Nut Muffins

MAKES 18 MUFFINS

Ada could not remember who had given her this recipe, but once she had it, she used it all through the cold weather months. Platters of Ada's piping hot muffins graced potluck suppers, harvest breakfasts, pre-Thanksgiving get-togethers, and many other social occasions, including lingering winter family breakfasts.

1 CUP ALL-PURPOSE FLOUR
1 CUP GRAHAM FLOUR
1 TABLESPOON BAKING POWDER
½ CUP SUGAR
1 TEASPOON SALT
½ CUP WALNUT MEATS, BROKEN
INTO COARSE PIECES

1 EGG, WELL BEATEN
1 CUP MILK, WARMED TO ROOM
TEMPERATURE
¼ CUP MELTED BUTTER

Preheat oven to 425°F. Thoroughly grease 18 muffin cups (if you have medium 12-cup pans, fill 18 cups with muffin batter, and remaining 6 cups ¼ full of water to prevent buckling).

Into a large bowl sift both white and graham flour with baking powder, sugar, and salt, then sift again. Fold in walnuts. Combine egg, milk, and melted butter. Make a well in the dry ingredients. Pour the egg mixture into the well; beat only long enough to form a soft dough. Spoon into prepared muffin pans.

Bake until well risen, golden brown, and firm to the touch, about 25 minutes. Serve piping hot with or without butter and sweet spreads.

THIS BREAD OF LIFE

Here in the corner window,
I bow my head over the hospital tray.
The cafeteria whispers
with the anxious tensions of 2 a.m.
The lights of the boulevard below the hill
spread arteries
where pulsing drops of car lights
thread lifelines through the night.

I pray, O Lord, that I may
be equal to my chosen profession,
to the path in which You have led me;
that I may be
all the nurse I have studied to be,
part of Your pattern of mercy
and healing.

I pray that the man in ICU
will make it through this night.
I pray that the young parents
waiting in peds
will see their child awaken.

When my shift is over, dear Lord,
please guide me home
safely through the dawn.

And now in this moment I thank you
for my calling
and for this bread of life.

ALVIN REISS

The Rosy Light of Dawn

KATHY, MY SISTER'S DAUGHTER, IS A KIND AND LOVING YOUNG WOMAN. AT EIGHTEEN, AFTER GRADUATING FROM HIGH SCHOOL, SHE CHOSE TO WORK IN CONVALESCENT HOSPITALS. THROUGH THE YEARS WE HAVE WATCHED HER GROW, NOTED THE SKILL AND STRENGTH THAT HAVE BECOME HERS, AND ADMIRED HER EAGERNESS TO CONTINUE HER EDUCATION SO THAT IN TIME SHE MAY BECOME AN R.N.

OTHERS TELL US OF HER GENEROSITY, THE WAY SHE SHARES HERSELF WITH PATIENTS, HOW SHE ENRICHES THEIR LIVES AND CHEERS THEM WITH HER SPECIAL SPUNKY SORT OF HUMOR, AND EASES, WHEN SHE CAN, THEIR PASSAGE THROUGH THE VEIL OF TIME.

SAFELY THROUGH THE NIGHT

*K*athy from an early age was a very tender, compassionate child, who so admired the story of Florence Nightingale that she copied out of an encyclopedia all she could about this famous English nurse, the founder of modern nursing methods and the heroine of the Crimean War.

Most of all she loved to tell her family how Florence Nightingale made the rounds of the hospital, carrying a lamp, bringing light into the darkness, as she passed along four miles of beds. She would smile at one soldier, say a few words of comfort to another. The grateful men called her "the lady with the lamp."

Lemon Biscuits

2 CUPS ALL-PURPOSE FLOUR

2 TEASPOONS BAKING POWDER

½ TEASPOON SALT

¼ CUP BUTTER OR SHORTENING,
   CHILLED

3 TEASPOONS GRATED LEMON RIND

⅔ CUP MILK

¼ CUP SUGAR

¼ TEASPOON LEMON JUICE

⅓ CUP MELTED BUTTER

MAKES 2½ DOZEN

Aunt Peg introduced the recipe for these delightful breakfast biscuits. Uncle Ben thought they were a bit fancy, but that didn't stop him from eating half a dozen with his eggs and coffee.

Preheat oven to 450°F. Set out and thoroughly grease three 12-cup medium muffin pans.

Into a medium bowl sift flour once; add baking powder and salt and sift a second time. Using a pastry cutter or fingertips, cut or work fat into the flour mixture. Add 1½ teaspoons lemon rind; blend well. Add milk all at once; stir just until flour is evenly dampened and a soft dough is formed. Turn onto a lightly floured surface; knead less than a minute, turning about 5 times. Roll ¼ inch thick, and cut with a 1½-inch floured biscuit cutter.

In a small bowl, combine sugar, remaining 1½ teaspoons lemon rind, and enough lemon juice to make a crumbly texture. Place half of the biscuits in prepared muffin cups; spread with melted butter and with sugar mixture. Top with remaining biscuit dough and press lightly together.

Bake until well risen, golden brown, and firm to the touch, 8 to 10 minutes. Remove from oven. Serve piping hot.

A Simple French Omelet

MAKES 1 SERVING

In our family, we often served this light breakfast dish with ½ pear (home-canned or store-bought) and Lemon Biscuits (page 81) with sweet butter. Our night-shift workers all swore they could eat it and go right to sleep.

1 TABLESPOON BUTTER OR
    VEGETABLE OIL
2 EGGS
2 TABLESPOONS MILK

¼ TEASPOON SALT
DASH OF PEPPER (NOT MORE THAN
    ⅛ TEASPOON)
¼ CUP MINCED HAM

Melt butter in a heavy iron frying pan. Beat eggs just enough to blend well. Add milk, salt, and pepper. Turn the pan from side to side until fat covers bottom and sides. Turn heat down to low and pour eggs into pan; let eggs stand for 1 minute. As soon as bubbles begin to form, lift edges of omelet with a spatula so that uncooked portion of eggs runs down and forms a rather smooth, creamy mass.

When omelet is nearly cooked, top one half with minced ham and roll the other half over onto it. Let stand a few minutes, then turn onto a hot plate. Serve immediately.

FISHERMEN

Dear God,
great Lord of loaves and fishes,
we cast our nets into the sea
as Simon Peter did at Galilee,
and through thy grace
fill our boats with your silver bounty,
food for our families and friends.
Ever thankful
we cast our nets again and again.
Bless our effort. Let us earn our bread
and live our lives as fishermen.

ALVIN REISS

BLESSINGS ON THE *KANDY DEE*

For years, our neighbor Hank Dillard worked in the woods. When layoffs came he took work cutting down "widow makers"—fallen trees that were tangled among the limbs of standing trees. Each year his wife, Kandy, was afraid that limbs might break and drop the remaining tree on him. She spoke to him of her fear, and Hank continued with his dangerous work, arguing that the family needed money to live on.

Then in the spring of fifty-four, Hank sold almost everything they had to buy a fishing boat, which he named the *Kandy Dee.* He moved his family over to the coast, telling Kandy that he would work at anything until the fishing business paid off. Several years later he had made enough money to finish paying off the loan he had taken out on the boat.

That winter, storms raged and waves lashed the coastline from Seattle to Coos Bay, damaging anchored fishing boats. Hank went out into the storm two or three times a day to check on the boat. Every time he returned to the house he would tell Kandy that no real damage had been done. Then, after a particularly savage storm blew in, he stayed with the boat. Late in the day, he watched the weather break, the dark clouds dissipate, and the sun break through. The wind laid.

Kandy was washing dishes and cleaning up the kitchen when he came in. At first she thought he was sick. Then, with glistening tears in his light blue eyes, he told her, "She made it through, I don't know why, but it passed over her."

Oven Fried Fillets with Homemade Tartar Sauce

MAKES 6 SERVINGS

Our friend Kandy calls this an everyday recipe, one that can be used with many different fish fillets. She recommends fillet of sole, silver salmon, snapper, cod, or lake trout.

2 POUNDS FISH FILLETS
1½ TEASPOONS SALT
½ CUP MILK
¼ TEASPOON BLACK PEPPER
1 CUP LIGHT-COLORED, DRY BREAD CRUMBS

¼ CUP MELTED BUTTER OR MARGARINE
HOMEMADE TARTAR SAUCE (RECIPE FOLLOWS)

Preheat oven to 475°F. Place an oven rack so that it is slightly above the middle of the oven. Set out and thoroughly grease a 13x9x2-inch baking pan.

Cut small fillets into 6 serving portions. *Note:* If fillets are large or thick, cut into serving-size pieces. In a small bowl combine salt and milk; stir to blend. Dip pieces of fish one at a time into the salted milk; dust lightly with black pepper; coat with bread crumbs one piece at a time. Place fillets in prepared baking pan. Pour melted butter over fish.

Bake until pieces are light brown and fish flakes easily when tested with a fork, 12 to 14 minutes. *Note:* Do not turn or baste.

Homemade Tartar Sauce

MAKES 1 CUP

1 CUP MAYONNAISE
2 TABLESPOONS FINELY CHOPPED DILL PICKLE
1 TABLESPOON MINCED PARSLEY

2 TEASPOONS FINELY CHOPPED PIMIENTO
1 TEASPOON MINCED CHIVES

Combine all ingredients in a small bowl. Blend together, cover, and chill until needed.

Kedgeree

2 CUPS COOKED RICE

4 HARD-COOKED EGGS, CHOPPED

2 CUPS COOKED FISH, FLAKED
(FRESH POACHED SALMON
PREFERRED)

½ CUP LIGHT CREAM

3 TABLESPOONS MINCED PARSLEY

SALT AS DESIRED (NOT MORE THAN
1 TEASPOON)

PEPPER AS DESIRED (NOT MORE
THAN ⅛ TEASPOON)

MAKES 6 SERVINGS

Aunt Alice taught Mother how to make this famous English breakfast dish. She served it hot or cold for lunch or supper, often with a simple green salad.

In the top of a double boiler, combine ingredients. Warm thoroughly over medium heat to serving temperature. Serve at once.

Easy-to-Make Creamed Oysters

2 TABLESPOONS BUTTER (NO
SUBSTITUTE)

2 TABLESPOONS ALL-PURPOSE
FLOUR

1 CUP THIN CREAM (HALF AND HALF
WILL DO NICELY)

SALT AND PEPPER TO TASTE

1 PINT OYSTERS, DRAINED

4 SLICES WHOLE WHEAT BREAD

1 TABLESPOON MINCED PARSLEY

MAKES 4 SERVINGS

These old-fashioned creamed oysters were often served as a brunchlike luncheon dish in homes where people left early in the morning to attend Thanksgiving service.

Heat the butter in a heavy-bottomed pan; add flour and stir until well blended. Add cream and stir until a smooth sauce forms. Add salt, pepper, and the oysters. The hot cream sauce should firm the oysters—do not cook longer. While oysters are firming up, make 4 pieces of whole wheat toast. Spoon sauce and oysters over toast and sprinkle with minced parsley. Serve immediately.

Note: Recipe may be doubled.

COLD-WEATHER COMPANY

*U*ncle Henry always said that storms and clear, cold weather brought folks together. I guess it's true, because by mid-November people we hadn't seen since the beginning of late fall harvest began to drop in for coffee, conversation, and cookies. Old men often stopped by, eager to share a good meal; women brought stews, casserole dishes, and baked goods.

The men would stoke the fire and find places near the stove to toast their cold feet and talk. Women preferred to sit at the table, sip coffee, gossip, and exchange recipes. Sheila and I, our cousins, and other children would sit on old quilts and play checkers or paper dolls. Some girls liked to play jacks on the bare floor. You could count on the boys, who were playing elsewhere, to tear in and out of the kitchen now and again, filling their hands and pockets with cookies.

By afternoon, early enough that families could get back home before dark, women would gather up their children and possessions, thank Mother for the good time, and bid their good-byes.

A BIT OF BACK BENDING

I intend to finish up before leaving to help
Betty pick up walnuts in her back yard. She has
a back problem and finds pain if she bends.
She always has picked them up and given to me,
so I feel it's time to go over and do a bit of
back bending myself.
The walnuts are lovely and large.
I helped her for a few hours and plan to go back
again on Saturday.

OPAL GUETZLAFF

Old-Country Beef Stew

5 ONIONS, CHOPPED

6 TABLESPOONS FAT

2 POUNDS BEEF, CUT INTO LONG
    STRIPS

½ TEASPOON SALT

⅛ TEASPOON BLACK PEPPER

2 TEASPOONS MARJORAM

1 MASHED CLOVE GARLIC

¾ CUP WHITE WINE

½ POUND BACON, CHOPPED

2 CUPS SOUR CREAM

MAKES 8 SERVINGS

Effie was given
this recipe by a
Hungarian woman
who had just
immigrated to this
country. In turn
Effie invited her and
her family to a
midwestern family
potluck.

In a large skillet or Dutch oven brown onions in fat; add meat, salt, pepper, marjoram, garlic, and wine. Simmer meat until it is almost tender, about 1 hour. In a separate skillet fry bacon until crisp. Drain. Add to meat mixture. Stir in sour cream and continue cooking until meat is tender, 25 to 30 minutes longer. Serve with Boiled Brown Rice (page 25) or Homemade Noodles (page 184).

Mother's Harvest Home Mincemeat Cookies

MAKES ABOUT 4 DOZEN
COOKIES

*This recipe is an old
one that Mother has
treasured since she
was a new bride,
some sixty-four years
ago. Each fall when
there is a nip in the
air, she takes out her
recipe and makes a
batch for the family
and one or two more
for cold-weather
company.*

1 CUP BUTTER

2 CUPS SUGAR

3 EGGS, WELL BEATEN

3 CUPS ALL-PURPOSE FLOUR

1 CUP MINCEMEAT, LACED WITH 2
   TABLESPOONS BRANDY

1 TEASPOON BAKING SODA

1 TEASPOON FRESHLY GRATED
   NUTMEG

½ TEASPOON GROUND CLOVES

⅛ TEASPOON GROUND GINGER

½ CUP WALNUTS, FINELY CHOPPED

Preheat oven to 375°F. Thoroughly grease a large baking sheet.
Set aside.

In a large mixing bowl cream butter and sugar together.
When light, add eggs, 1 cup flour, and the mincemeat. Sift remaining flour with baking soda and spices. Turn flour mixture,
all at once, into the butter-mincemeat mixture. Stir until a stiff
dough is formed (it should be almost stiff enough to roll). If you
are using moist homemade mincemeat, a little more flour may
be needed. Drop heaping teaspoonfuls of dough about 2 inches
apart on the prepared baking sheet.

Bake until cookies are well risen, browned, and firm to the
touch, 15 to 18 minutes.

ON THE SUNNY SIDE

*Hear the clacking guinea;
Hear the cattle moo;
Hear the horses whinny,
Looking out at you!
On the hitching block, boys,
Grandly satisfied.
See the old peacock, boys,
On the sunny side!*

JAMES WHITCOMB RILEY
Songs of Summer

LATE FALL HARVEST POTLUCK

*A*bout two weeks before Thanksgiving, neighbors and friends in our area usually got together for a potluck supper. Young folks invited older neighbors, picking them up for the party and taking them home afterward. Women came with casserole dishes, pies, and salads. Mae Dalton roasted a huge tom turkey. Men brought a little wine and cold drinks for women and children, and Lena made more than one pot of coffee and several of tea.

The year the potluck was held at our house, neighbors new and old came to wish us a happy holiday season and share in the potluck. Some who had not been specifically invited heard about it through others and came with food and folding chairs. The new neighbors arrived and said, "Charlie told us to bring a dish and be at your house by six o'clock." We welcomed them at the door, shook their hands, and told them we were glad they had come.

The dinner was a smashing success. The women had outdone themselves. Men and boys kept sampling this and that, all the while complaining that they were eating too much. And women shared with each other bits of food that were left over. It was nearly one o'clock in the morning when the last car eased down our driveway.

When it was all over I couldn't even count how many of our neighbors had told us good night and wished us a happy Thanksgiving.

Mae Dalton's Roast Turkey with Easy-to-Make Sausage Stuffing and Golden Glow Gravy

MAKES ABOUT 2 SERVINGS PER POUND WITH SOME LEFT OVER

Women with large families, like Mae, often roasted twenty-pound birds for holiday dinners at home. But for neighborhood potlucks they usually roasted several twelve-to-fifteen-pound birds. They knew, because of age and size, these smaller birds would be tender and would yield about two servings per pound. They didn't use smaller turkeys since those under twelve pounds were thought to yield too few—only 1⅓—servings per pound.

THAWING A FROZEN TURKEY

In order to retain the most moisture possible, thaw a frozen turkey in its opened or punctured bag on a tray in the refrigerator for 2 to 4 days. Or leave the turkey in its wrappings and set it in cool water. The bird should be soaked in its plastic container; without it some of its flavor soaks away. If the bird must be thawed quickly, put it in several shopping bags and allow it to thaw at room temperature for 5 to 6 hours. The brown bags keep the surface temperature cool. Remove the giblets as soon as they are thawed enough to break free, and put them in a separate containers, the liver in one and the neck and gizzard in another.

Note: To prevent food poisoning, do not stuff a bird before freezing it and don't stuff a bird the night before roasting it.

ABOUT COOKING GIBLETS

To prepare giblets, cover the heart, gizzard, and neck, if you wish, with water and simmer in a covered saucepan until tender. When done, take the pan off the heat; remove giblets with a slotted spoon and dice them. Reserve stock and combine with diced giblets (and neck meat) to use in a flavorful gravy or for moistening dressing.

Note: Discard liver or pan fry it.

ROASTING THE TURKEY

Rub the bird with butter and then rub into it salt, pepper, and marjoram. Use 1 teaspoon salt, ¼ teaspoon pepper, and ¼ teaspoon marjoram per pound of meat. Let the turkey set overnight in a cool place to allow flavors to blend. The following day, stuff it with onions, celery, garlic, and apples. Put the turkey breast side down on a rack in a shallow roasting pan.

Roast in a moderate oven (350°F), allowing 20 to 25 minutes per pound. Baste frequently with the fat that gathers in the bottom of the pan. Spoon some of the fat into the cavity to baste the breast, or put a cube of margarine in with the stuffing. When cooking time is about half over, turn the bird breast side up and continue roasting until it is golden brown.

Test for doneness with a meat thermometer, sticking it inside the thigh near the hip bone or groin. This is the slowest-cooking part of the turkey. A temperature of 170–180°F here means the bird is fully cooked. If no thermometer is available, test for doneness by pressing the drumstick. If the turkey is done, the meat will feel soft and the drumstick should twist out of the joint. The meat will also have shrunk up the bone so that the joint where the foot was removed will be bare.

A turkey carves better if allowed to set for 15 to 20 minutes after it is removed from the oven. Serve while hot with Easy-to-Make Sausage Stuffing (recipe follows), vegetables, and Golden Glow Gravy (page 167).

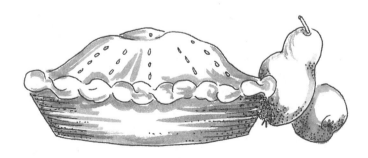

Easy-to-Make Sausage Stuffing

MAKES 24 SERVINGS	1 POUND LEAN, SEASONED FRESH PORK SAUSAGE	2 QUARTS WHITE OR GOLDEN EGG BREAD, TORN OR CUT INTO SMALL PIECES
	1¼ CUPS FINELY CHOPPED ONION	1 TABLESPOON SALT, MORE AS DESIRED
	6 CUPS COARSELY CHOPPED CELERY	2 TEASPOONS BLACK PEPPER
	⅔ CUP BUTTER OR MARGARINE, SOFTENED AT ROOM TEMPERATURE	2 TABLESPOONS PULVERIZED OREGANO LEAVES
	4 QUARTS MIXED SPECIALTY BREADS—RYE, WHOLE WHEAT, ETC.—TORN OR CUT INTO SMALL PIECES	1 TABLESPOON GARLIC GRANULES
		4½ CUPS OR MORE CHICKEN STOCK, OR WATER SEASONED WITH CHICKEN SOUP BASE (MILK MAY BE USED)

Prepare stuffing while turkey is roasting. In a large skillet crumble and fry sausage until fat is rendering out and meat is about half-done. Drain off fat. Then add onion, celery, butter, and a cup or more of hot water. Simmer until onions and celery are clear and tender-done but not browned.

Meanwhile, put pieces of bread into a very large bowl. Pour over them the contents of the skillet. Add salt, pepper, oregano, and garlic granules. Pour liquid over bread mixture and stir to blend. *Stuffing should be rather moist—if the mixture is too dry the stuffing will lose its succulence.*

About 40 to 45 minutes before turkey is done, set the pan or pans of stuffing in the oven to bake. If you don't have room to bake the turkey and stuffing at the same time, prepare stuffing and bake earlier in the day. When needed, warm to a moderately hot serving temperature.

Ada's Honey Candied Yams

MAKES 6 TO 8 SERVINGS	4 TO 6 MEDIUM YAMS	A SPRINKLING OF SALT
	⅔ CUP WARMED HONEY (CLOVER PREFERRED)	½ TEASPOON FRESHLY GRATED NUTMEG
	½ CUP MELTED BUTTER	

Preheat oven to 300° or 325°F. Thoroughly butter a 13x9x2-inch baking dish; set aside.

Wash yams, then in a large kettle cook them in salted water to cover. When done but still firm, drain, peel, and cut yams into quarters. Arrange lengthwise in layers in prepared baking dish, spooning honey over each layer. Pour the melted butter over all and sprinkle on a little salt and a dusting of nutmeg.

Bake uncovered for about 1½ to 1¾ hours.

These honey- and butter-candied yams are delicious when topped with a dusting of freshly ground nutmeg. Old Uncle, who lived down the road from Ada, loved them and could make a whole meal of them, topped off with a cold glass or two of icy fresh milk.

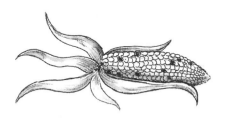

Easy-to-Make Corn Soufflé

1 TABLESPOON BUTTER OR MARGARINE	⅛ TEASPOON BLACK PEPPER	MAKES 4 TO 6 SERVINGS
1 TABLESPOON FLOUR	1 MEDIUM JAR PIMIENTOS	
½ CUP MILK	2 CUPS CORN PULP	
1 TEASPOON SALT	2 EGGS, SEPARATED: YOLKS BEATEN TO A FROTH, WHITES BEATEN INTO STIFF PEAKS	
¼ TEASPOON PAPRIKA		

Preheat oven to 375°F. Thoroughly grease a 1- or 1½-quart casserole dish.

To make thin white sauce, blend in a small saucepan over low heat butter and flour. Stir constantly; cook until smooth and bubbly. Remove from heat. Add milk, salt, paprika, and pepper. Heat to boiling, stirring constantly. Boil for 1 minute.

Rub pimientos through a sieve and add them to the sauce. Stir in the corn. Cool slightly, then add beaten yolks and fold in stiffly beaten egg whites.

Turn into prepared baking dish. Set dish in a pan of hot water. Bake until eggs are set, about 30 minutes.

When the last of the fresh corn is brought to the house, the women in our family shuck and trim the corncobs. Then, with a sharp knife, they cut halfway through the kernels, leaving half on the cob. They cook the loose kernels in a small amount of water for supper, then scrape the remaining pulp off the cob for corn soufflé.

Cabbage, Apple, and Carrot Salad with Ella's Cooked Salad Dressing

MAKES 8 OR MORE SERVINGS

Ella's delicious all-purpose salad dressing can be used in so many ways: to dress salads like this one, spooned over hot or cold vegetables, or stirred into potato or macaroni salads. It is a fine old-time dressing with an old-fashioned zest.

1 SMALL HEAD CABBAGE, TRIMMED AND FINELY CHOPPED

2 LARGE APPLES, PEELED, CORED, AND CHOPPED (GOLDEN DELICIOUS PREFERRED)

2 LARGE CARROTS, PEELED AND COARSELY GRATED

ELLA'S COOKED SALAD DRESSING (RECIPE FOLLOWS)

1 LARGE SPRIG OF PARSLEY FOR GARNISH

In a large bowl combine cabbage, apples, and carrots; add enough dressing to moisten vegetables. Turn into an attractive serving dish and garnish with the parsley (sprinkle minced leaves over the top or press small clusters into center or around edges of salad).

Ella's Cooked Salad Dressing

MAKES ABOUT 1¾ CUPS

2 EGG YOLKS

1 TEASPOON SALT

1 TEASPOON DRY MUSTARD

PINCH OF RED PEPPER (LESS THAN ⅛ TEASPOON)

2 TABLESPOONS CIDER VINEGAR

2 TABLESPOONS LEMON JUICE, STRAINED

1 TABLESPOON SUGAR

1 CUP OLIVE OIL

1 CUP WATER

⅓ CUP CORNSTARCH

1 TABLESPOON BUTTER

Make salad dressing an hour or more before assembling salad and chill until needed.

Put egg yolks, salt, mustard, red pepper, vinegar, lemon juice, and sugar into a medium bowl. Pour over the olive oil. *Do not stir.*

In the top of a double boiler, combine water, cornstarch, and butter; cook over boiling water until smooth and thick, about 10 minutes. Stir occasionally. Remove from heat. While still hot, pour thickened water mixture over the other ingredients. Beat with rotary or electric mixer until dressing has a light-bodied, smooth texture.

Mother's Potato Refrigerator Rolls

2 PACKAGES GRANULATED YEAST

1½ CUPS WARM WATER (105 TO 115°F)

⅔ CUP SUGAR

1½ TEASPOONS SALT

⅔ CUP BUTTER OR MARGARINE, SOFTENED AT ROOM TEMPERATURE, PLUS 2 TO 3

TABLESPOONS FOR BRUSHING TOPS OF ROLLS

2 EGGS, BEATEN TO A FROTH

1 CUP LUKEWARM MASHED POTATOES

7 CUPS FLOUR, PLUS ½ CUP OR MORE FOR KNEADING

MAKES ABOUT 2 DOZEN

Mother loved to make rolls for get-togethers, reunions, and holidays. She especially liked this simple recipe. Once made, the dough can be stored in an airtight container in the refrigerator at 45°F for about 10 days. It can also be baked all at once in rolls or small loaves. Much to our delight, when making these for company, Mother often pinched off a small panful of rolls and baked them for our supper.

Thoroughly grease a 13x9x2-inch baking pan. In a small bowl soften yeast in warm water.

Pour yeast and water into a large bowl and combine with sugar, salt, butter, eggs, potatoes, and 4 cups of flour. Beat with a wooden spoon until a thick batter has formed. Add enough remaining flour to make a dough that is easy to handle, then turn onto a lightly floured surface. Knead until smooth and elastic, 5 to 8 minutes.

Wash large mixing bowl, rinse, dry, and thoroughly grease. Put dough in prepared bowl; turn greased side up. Cover tightly and refrigerate for 8 to 12 hours. The following morning, remove dough from refrigerator, punch down, then pinch into buns the size of large eggs. Place in prepared pan. Brush tops with butter. Let rise until double in bulk, about 1½ hours.

Meanwhile, heat oven to 400°F. Bake until rolls are well puffed, lightly browned, and firm to the touch, 15 to 20 minutes.

Sheila's Southern Sweet Potato Pie with Spiced Whipped Cream

MAKES ONE 9-INCH PIE

This old-time pie is a favorite at harvest home suppers or family reunions. At our house we serve it topped with Spiced Whipped Cream.

SINGLE CRUST PASTRY PLUS (PAGE 12)

2 CUPS BOILED SWEET POTATOES, PEELED AND MASHED

¾ CUP FIRMLY PACKED GOLDEN BROWN SUGAR

1 TEASPOON CINNAMON

½ TEASPOON FRESHLY GRATED NUTMEG

½ TEASPOON GINGER

½ TEASPOON SALT

2 EGGS, WELL BEATEN

1⅔ CUPS RICH MILK OR LIGHT CREAM

1 TABLESPOON VANILLA

SPICED WHIPPED CREAM (RECIPE FOLLOWS)

Preheat oven to 425°F. Set out a deep-dish 9-inch pie pan. Make pastry, roll it out, and line pan, leaving 1-inch overhang. Tuck overlapping dough under rim of pastry shell. Flute edge. Bake pie shell in hot oven for 15 minutes to set the crust.

In a large bowl combine sweet potatoes, brown sugar, cinnamon, nutmeg, ginger, and salt. When thoroughly blended, add eggs, milk or cream, and vanilla. Stir until smooth. To prevent spills, set pie pan on oven rack and carefully pour filling into the pie shell. Bake for 15 minutes.

Reduce temperature to 350°F. Bake until knife inserted in center comes out clean, about 45 minutes. When done, remove pie from oven and set on a wire rack to cool. Serve with Spiced Whipped Cream.

Spiced Whipped Cream

1 CUP HEAVY CREAM

¼ CUP SUGAR

⅛ TEASPOON FRESHLY GRATED NUTMEG

1 TEASPOON BRANDY OR BRANDY FLAVORING

MAKES 2⅓ CUPS

Beat cream until fluffed and mounded. Add sugar a little at a time, beating after each addition. Fold in nutmeg and brandy or brandy flavoring until blended. Continue beating as necessary until cream is glossy. For thicker cream, beat a little longer (overwhipping will make the cream taste greasy).

From TIME OF CLEARER TWITTERINGS

Of the days of long ago,
When the stream seemed thus and so
In our boyish eyes: — The bank
Greener then, through rank on rank
Of the mottled sycamores,
Touching tops across the shores:

Here, the hazel thicket stood —
There, the almost pathless wood
Where the shellbark hickory tree
Rained its wealth on you and me.
Autumn! as you loved us then,
Take us to your heart again!

JAMES WHITCOMB RILEY

Forever in Our
Hearts Remembering

WHEN, AS A CHILD, LIFE SOMETIMES SEEMED MORE THAN I COULD BEAR, I WOULD GO THROUGH THE WALNUT ORCHARD AND THE GATE THAT LED TO AUNT MABEL'S HOUSE. ONE SUCH TIME, SHE TALKED TO ME ABOUT A CHILD THAT LIVES WITHIN US ALL WHOSE MEMORIES SHAPE OUR ADULT LIVES. THIS CHILD SUFFERS STILL THE SORROWS AND FEARS OF THE PAST, AND THIS CHILD'S HEART IS STILL ALIVE IN US, ECHOING THE SOUND OF BABY LAUGHTER, THE LISPING VOICE OF A TODDLER, THE UNSPOKEN VIGOR OF A RAMBUNCTIOUS LITTLE BOY——A DAREDEVIL AND ANGEL ALL IN ONE.

AS AUNT MABEL AND I WALKED THROUGH HER YARD, LISTENING TO THE PEACOCKS AND GUINEA HENS CRY OUT, SHE PUT HER ARM AROUND ME AND TOLD ME THAT IT ISN'T EASY TO GROW UP, TO BE TWELVE YEARS OLD. SHE HUGGED ME AND SAID, "JANIE, ALWAYS REMEMBER THAT WHO YOU WERE STRONGLY INFLUENCES WHO YOU BECOME. HOLD FAST TO THE CHILD WITHIN YOU FOR I KNEW HER THEN AND NOW, AND SHE IS A KIND AND LOVING CHILD."

JEWELS FROM THE COOL, DARK CELLAR

*M*other well remembers, as do other midwestern folk, the cyclones. Their dark, fast-moving clouds and galelike winds sent shingles flying off the roofs, turned hens' feathers inside out, and had children running this way and that, followed by drenched mothers and fathers who shooed them into the safety of the root cellar.

IN THE LAP OF THE EARTH

Down in the root cellar
'twas scary and dark
but it hid us from cyclones
while the matches did spark.

Potatoes, carrots and apples
hid with us too
until the roar of the wind
at last bid us adieu.

PATRICIA PARISH KUHN

Honey Baked Apples

MAKES 6 SERVINGS

Even after he had bought himself a Model T Ford, Uncle Ned would stop by the family homes on Saturday mornings with his cart drawn by Ginger, his old palomino mare. Ginger would stand patiently waiting for him, nudging him now and again and watching him as he dug around in his well-used vegetable cart for freshly picked apples, a few squash, and honey—gifts for his neighbors. Then, after getting a thank you and a hug from the womenfolk and an apple for Ginger, he would go on his way.

6 FIRM BAKING APPLES

¾ CUP HONEY

1 CUP WATER

1 TABLESPOON BUTTER

COLD, SWEET CREAM AS DESIRED FOR SPOONING OVER BAKED APPLES

Preheat oven to 350°F. Set out and lightly grease an 8 or 9x11x2-inch layer cake pan.

Wash and core the apples. Peel about ⅓ of the way down from the stem end so the apples won't burst while baking.

Arrange apples in pan, pared side up. Boil honey, water, and butter together for 10 minutes; pour over the apples. Bake until tender and lightly colored and the syrup, which should be spooned over the apples several times during baking, has thickened. Serve with or without cold, sweet cream.

Aunt Sue's Cherry Tarts

1 QUART TART CANNED CHERRIES	FLAKY SINGLE CRUST PASTRY	MAKES 8 SERVINGS
SUGAR AS NEEDED	(RECIPE FOLLOWS)	
¼ CUP CORNSTARCH	WHIPPED CREAM OR VANILLA ICE	
¼ TEASPOON SALT	CREAM AS DESIRED	

Preheat oven to 350°F. Open 1 quart of preferably home-canned pie cherries. Pour the juice into a saucepan. Put the cherries in a bowl and remove the pits. Put the saucepan onto medium heat, adding sugar only if the cherries are too tart. When the juice boils, add the cornstarch, which has been moistened with a little water, and the salt. Cook, stirring constantly, until thickened. Turn off the heat. Add the drained cherries and blend. Set aside to cool.

Make the pastry. Roll it into a 12-inch circle. Cut out 8 circles, each 4½ inches in diameter. Turn an 8-cup muffin tin over and fit each circle over the convex bottom of a cup (pleat as necessary for a smooth fit). Prick with a fork. Bake until pastry is crisp and lightly browned. Remove from oven and cool.

When cool, remove pastries from the pan and fill with ½ cup of cherry filling. Serve plain, with a tablespoon of whipped cream, or with a small scoop of ice cream.

When Aunt Sue and Uncle Bud bought the farm, they planted six sweet cherry trees, among them Bing, Royal Ann, and Black Tartarian. They also had six pie cherry trees, including the tart and tangy North Star, Meteor, and Montmorency varieties. Through the years Aunt Sue has baked these firm cherries in countless turnovers, cobblers, and crisps.

Flaky Single Crust Pastry

1 CUP ALL-PURPOSE FLOUR, PLUS	½ TEASPOON SALT	MAKES ONE
FLOUR FOR ROLLING OUT	½ CUP BUTTER	9-INCH PIE CRUST
DOUGH	2 TO 4 TABLESPOONS COLD WATER	

Preheat oven to 450°F. Sift the flour and salt together into a large bowl. Cut in the butter using a pastry blender or two dinner knives, or rub butter into the flour with your fingertips until all pieces of dough are the size of small peas. Gradually sprinkle just enough water to hold the pastry together, mixing lightly and quickly with a fork after each addition. (This leads to a flakier piecrust.) Turn onto a floured surface and form pastry into a ball.

Effie's Late Fall Deep Dish Pear Pie

MAKES 6 SERVINGS

Most of the women in the family stored several boxes of Bosc pears in the cellar, bringing them out to ripen in the kitchen only as they were needed for pies or crisps.

FLAKY SINGLE CRUST PASTRY (PAGE 101)

5 CUPS PEELED, CORED, SLICED PEARS

JUICE OF 1 LEMON, STRAINED

½ TEASPOON SALT

1 TABLESPOON ALL-PURPOSE FLOUR

¼ TEASPOON NUTMEG

1 TEASPOON CINNAMON

1 CUP SUGAR OR LESS, DEPENDING ON SWEETNESS OF PEARS

2 TABLESPOONS BUTTER

CHILLED HEAVY CREAM TO SPOON OVER PIE AS DESIRED

Preheat oven to 425°F. Make the pastry and chill dough.

Arrange one layer of pears (which have been sprinkled with lemon juice) in a large, flat baking dish. Combine salt, flour, nutmeg, cinnamon, and sugar. Sprinkle ½ over first layer; add another layer of pears, and sprinkle a second time. Dot butter over the top.

Roll out the pastry into a shape that will completely cover the prepared dish. Fit it to the top of the baking dish; trim and crimp as desired. Cut vent holes in the top and bake until the crust is golden brown and the pears are tender when pierced with a skewer, about 45 minutes.

Remove from the oven. These may be eaten hot or cold, with or without chilled cream spooned over them.

Note: Some varieties of pears are so sweet that they do not need sugar when baked.

From Old Homes

These old places by the road are treasure houses of
delight
To those who enter them with seeing eyes:
Here is the parlor, where in years gone by
The best rag carpet spread its gaudy widths
Over the fresh new straw that crackled underneath;
Yonder, the bedroom where the old four-poster stood,
And oft the good wife drew its rope-springs taut,
As more and more they sagged and pulled awry
Beneath the weight of sturdy growing boys.
Here is the kitchen where on baking days
The fat and bursting loaves of golden bread
Sifted their odorous steam across the window sill
To nostrils keen in scent of homely, tempting food;
Here, too, the apple-butter sputtered on the red-hot
stove,
And chickens lay in state deep in the oven's maw,
Yielding their rich aroma to the air.

GRACE E. HALL
Patchwork

OLD-FASHIONED COUNTRY FARE

*W*hen I was a girl at home, we lived off what we raised: beef, chicken for meat and eggs, berries from Grandpa's raspberry and strawberry patches, vegetables from huge gardens, the milk from our cows, and more. Our trips to the store were for staples only.

Mother cooked mostly with what she had on hand, as did other women in the family. Being raised on the farm as they were, they learned to be self-sufficient. They were frugal, hardworking homemakers. They thought of themselves as the heart of the family. Everything was organized about the home: Children learned values and morals, and that everyone had to do his share. Children were taught at their mother's knee that schooling was vital to a good life, that God's way taught them to be honest, compassionate, kind, and loving.

We all contributed to the work on the farm. Even my little sister, Sheila, gathered eggs, dried the dishes, helped Grandpa pick berries, and sometimes mopped the kitchen floor. There was an efficiency to family life; you could count on meals being well prepared and wholesome and your school lunch pail being filled with things you liked. There was a good Sunday dinner after church, with or without company.

Looking back, I know such a life is very old-fashioned and simple, but it was warm, well put together, filled with those you loved and blessings rare.

Great-Grandma's Beef Pie

MAKES 6 SERVINGS

After a Sunday dinner or harvest supper, every household in the family made leftover beef roast or boiled beef into a meat pie. Each lady topped it to suit herself. Effie stirred up an herbed biscuit dough; Great-Grandma preferred lard or butter pastry; Aunt Mabel had already switched in the thirties to shortening.

FILLING
2 CUPS ROASTED OR BOILED BEEF, CHOPPED
1 CUP DICED POTATOES
½ CUP DICED ONION
½ CUP DICED CARROTS
½ CUP DICED CELERY

1½ CUPS LEFTOVER BEEF GRAVY
SALT AND PEPPER TO TASTE

PASTRY
1 CUP FLOUR
½ TEASPOON SALT
½ CUP LARD OR BUTTER
COLD WATER TO MIX PASTRY

Preheat oven to 400°F. Set out and lightly grease a deep, oven-proof casserole.

In a medium bowl combine meat, vegetables, gravy, salt, and pepper. Turn into prepared casserole dish.

In a medium bowl sift flour with salt. Using a pastry blender, cut the lard or butter into the flour mixture; add enough cold water, 1 tablespoon at a time, to the flour-lard or flour-butter mixture to form a stiff dough. Roll out the pastry and cut it to fit the top of the casserole dish. Flute the edges and bake for 20 minutes, then turn down the heat to 350°F and continue baking for another 30 minutes. Serve while still hot.

Aunt Mae's Sweet Potato Rusks

2 CUPS MILK (ONLY RAW MILK
NEED BE SCALDED;
PASTEURIZED MILK NEED
ONLY BE WARMED)

2 TABLESPOONS GRANULATED
YEAST

2 CUPS HOT MASHED SWEET
POTATOES

¼ CUP HONEY

¼ CUP BUTTER OR MARGARINE,
PLUS 2 OR MORE TABLE-
SPOONS FOR TOPS OF BAKED
RUSKS

1 TABLESPOON SALT

2 EGGS, WELL BEATEN

6 CUPS FLOUR, PLUS 1 CUP FOR
KNEADING AND SHAPING

MAKES 3 DOZEN OR
MORE

*Old-time cookbooks
are full of recipes for
making rusks—light,
soft, sweetened
biscuits or bread.
They can be twisted
into a spiral or made
into a roll. Ladies of
the day toasted
cooled rolls in the
oven or baked them
a second time until
they were brown
and crisp.*

In a small bowl, pour warm milk over yeast to soften it.

In a large bowl, thoroughly combine hot mashed sweet potatoes with honey, ¼ cup butter or margarine, and salt. Cool, then add eggs. Stir in the yeast-milk mixture. Add flour a little at a time, beating well after each addition. Turn out onto a lightly floured surface. Knead until a smooth, elastic dough, so soft it can barely be handled, is formed.

Thoroughly grease a second large bowl. Place dough in bowl; move it around until the surface of the ball of dough is greased; turn greased side up. Cover dough with damp kitchen towel; set in a warm place to double in bulk, about 45 minutes.

Meanwhile, preheat oven to 450°F. Turn risen dough out onto a lightly floured surface. Pinch into balls about the size of large eggs. Place on well-greased baking sheet, leaving a little space between each roll. Cover and let rise until tripled in bulk, 30 to 35 minutes.

Bake until rusks are well risen, golden brown, and firm to the touch, 12 to 15 minutes. To test for doneness, look at bottoms of rolls. If they are light-colored, the rusks are not yet baked through. Remove from oven and transfer to wire rack. While still hot, rub surface with butter or margarine to soften tops of rusks.

Uncle Ned's Buttered Jerusalem Artichokes

MAKES 4 SERVINGS

*Uncle Ned used to
say, "Once you plant
them durn turbers
you got 'em growin'
everywhere." He
therefore learned to
cook them this way
and that. Effie loved
them buttered, so she
made up this recipe
for him and gave him
a little pot of fresh
parsley and some
celery flakes she had
dried earlier in the
year to use in it.*

1 POUND JERUSALEM ARTICHOKES
2 TABLESPOONS BUTTER
⅔ CUP WATER
¼ TEASPOON CELERY FLAKES

1 TEASPOON LEMON JUICE,
   STRAINED
SALT AND PEPPER TO TASTE
1 TABLESPOON MINCED PARSLEY

Scrub tubers with a stiff brush under cold water. Put butter in a heavy frying pan. Slice the artichokes into the pan. Add water, celery flakes, and lemon juice. Cover tightly and cook until the artichokes are tender and the water has been absorbed. Season with salt, pepper, and parsley. Serve immediately.

Aunt Mabel's Cranberry Tea

MAKES 1 GALLON

*When our family
gathered for harvest
suppers, this tea,
along with icy milk
and steaming coffee,
was served by the
gallon. Mothers who
thought the beverage
was a "healthy drink"
thinned it with warm
or cold water for
small children.*

1½ CUPS SUGAR
6 WHOLE CLOVES
2 CUPS ORANGE JUICE, STRAINED

JUICE OF 1 LEMON, STRAINED
1 POUND FRESH CRANBERRIES
1 QUART GINGER ALE (OPTIONAL)

In a small saucepan dissolve sugar in 2 cups hot water. Add cloves. Boil to make a medium syrup. Cool slightly; remove cloves; add orange juice and lemon juice. In a large saucepan cover cranberries with 2 quarts water. Cook until soft. Crush and strain. In a 1-gallon pan or bowl combine sugar-citrus juice mixture with strained cranberry juice. Store in the refrigerator until needed. Just before serving, add 1 quart more water and heat to serving temperature or add 1 quart ginger ale and serve chilled.

SWEET TREATS

*W*hen my mother, aunts, and uncles were young, they had to make all their own sweet treats and their own entertainment. On late fall evenings the Meekins boys and girls would have a get-together with friends and provide the treats. Grandpa always stored apples, nuts, and popcorn in the cellar. The girls could all make various treats: cakes, buttered popcorn, popcorn balls, candied apples, a batch of fudge, divinity, taffy, or tutti frutti. As for entertainment, the boys got out the guitars and fiddles and played a little music.

Eventually, following a neighborhood custom, someone would take the phone off the hook so that friends along the party line could listen to some good old songs for a while. With Mother on the organ, the boys played "Over the Waves," "The Isle of Capri," and "Shall We Gather at the River" while the others ate and listened.

Sugared and Spiced Pecans

MAKES ABOUT 4 CUPS

Women of the thirties loved to make these crunchy fall treats. They are easy to make but don't last long, not when the men and young ones are sampling their way through the house.

1 TABLESPOON MELTED BUTTER OR MARGARINE

1 EGG WHITE, LIGHTLY BEATEN

2 CUPS UNROASTED PECAN HALVES (ABOUT 1 POUND OF UNSHELLED NUTS)

1 CUP SUGAR

½ TEASPOON SALT

1½ TEASPOONS CINNAMON

¾ TEASPOON GRATED NUTMEG

¾ TEASPOON ALLSPICE

Preheat oven to 300°F. Set out a 10x15 shallow baking sheet.

In a medium bowl slowly stir melted butter into egg white. Fold in nutmeats. In a small bowl combine sugar, salt, and spices. Spread about ¼ of the sugar mixture on baking sheet; cover nutmeats a few at a time with about ¼ of the mixture. Arrange on the sheet. Spread balance of nuts on baking sheet. Coat remaining nuts a few at a time with remaining sugar mixture.

Bake until nuts are lightly browned, 15 to 20 minutes. Remove nuts from oven; stir gently to separate them. Cool, then store in a tightly closed container (a glass jar with a tight-fitting lid will do nicely).

AMAZING GRACE

Amazing grace! how sweet the sound
That saved a wretch like me!
I once was lost, but now am found,
Was blind but now I see.

'Twas grace that taught my heart to fear,
And grace my fears relieved;
How precious did that grace appear
The hour I first believed!

Thro' many dangers, toils and snares,
I have already come;
'Tis grace hath brought me safe thus far,
And grace will lead me home.

When we've been there ten thousand years,
Bright shining as the sun,
We've no less days to sing God's praise
Than when we first begun.

JOHN NEWTON
Songs of Praise

An Unanswered Thanksgiving Day Prayer Fulfilled

WHEN INDIAN SUMMER IS GONE AND THERE IS A BITE IN THE AIR, MOTHER OFTEN TELLS US AGAIN ABOUT A BLESSING THAT CAME ON A THANKSGIVING LONG AGO:

IDA LOUISE AND HER HUSBAND, JACK, HAD CATTLE, APPLE ORCHARDS, ACRES OF WHEAT, A SMALL DAIRY, HOGS, AND SOME PRODUCE ON THEIR FARM. THEY LIVED IN A HUGE, WELL-KEPT OLD FIVE-BEDROOM HOUSE WITH THEIR CHILDREN, TWO GIRLS AND THREE BOYS WHO THE FAMILY ALWAYS SAID WERE CARBON COPIES OF JACK.

BUT THAT WASN'T REALLY TRUE. AUNT CLARY TOOK EVERY OPPORTUNITY TO REMIND THEM THAT EACH CHILD IS A GIFT FROM GOD, AN INDIVIDUAL WITH HIS OR HER OWN FLAWS AND PERFECTIONS, AND THAT EVEN TWINS ARE NOT LIKE PEAS IN A POD. PERHAPS THAT WAS WHY THE TRAGEDY CAME ABOUT.

YOUNG ROB, THE YOUNGEST SON, WAS NOT LIKE HIS BROTHERS. THEY,

LIKE THEIR FATHER, LOVED THE FARM AND WOULD WORK LONG HOURS ON IT DILIGENTLY AND WITH GUSTO. THEY SWEATED IN THE SUN AND, WHEN IT RAINED, SLOGGED THROUGH THE MUDDY FIELDS WITHOUT A COMPLAINT. ROB DID HIS CHORES WILLINGLY. HE BROUGHT THE COWS TO THE BARN, FED AND MILKED THEM, FED THE HOGS, STACKED HAY BALES, AND DID ANY OTHER CHORE ASSIGNED TO HIM WITHOUT COMMENT. BUT ROB'S REAL TALENTS LAY ELSEWHERE.

ROB SANG WITH HIS MOTHER IN THE CHOIR AND PLAYED OLD HYMNS ON HIS VIOLIN SO BEAUTIFULLY THAT TEARS CAME INTO THE EYES OF THE CONGREGATION. TOWNSPEOPLE ASKED HIM TO PLAY AND SING THE SONGS HE MADE UP ABOUT THE COUNTRY PEOPLE HE KNEW AND THE COUNTRYSIDE HE LOVED AT ALL SORTS OF EVENTS. THE NEIGHBORS SAID, "THAT ONE'S LIKE HIS MOTHER." AND, IN THE SMALL FARMING TOWN, PEOPLE TALKED ABOUT THE FAMILY, BUT NO ONE EVER SAID ANYTHING TO IDA LOUISE OR JACK.

THEN ONE DAY, WHEN HE WAS NOT QUITE SIXTEEN, ROB TOOK MONEY OUT OF HIS MOTHER'S COOKIE JAR, LEFT HER A NOTE, AND RAN AWAY. EVERYONE LOOKED FOR HIM. WOMEN QUIETLY AGREED THAT THEY'D BEEN WORRIED ABOUT HIM FOR SOME TIME, AND MEN HOPED TO FIND HIM AND TALK SOME SENSE INTO HIM. BUT EVEN HIS FRIENDS AND BROTHERS COULD NOT FIND HIM.

IDA LOUISE AND JACK WERE DEVASTATED. MEMBERS OF THE FAMILY PRAYED DAILY FOR HIS RETURN AND SAFETY. THE CHURCH HELD A SPECIAL SERVICE SO THAT COMMUNITY MEMBERS COULD ASK GOD FOR HIS RETURN. BUT YEARS PASSED AND PEOPLE STILL TALKED ABOUT THE LOSS OF A BOY LIKE ROB. THROUGH THE YEARS, ON THANKSGIVING DAY AFTER THE GRACE HAD BEEN SAID, THE FAMILY PRAYED FOR ROB'S RETURN OR AT LEAST HIS WELL-BEING.

IN 1938, THE WHOLE FAMILY—GRANDPARENTS, GRANDCHILDREN, AND GREAT-GRANDCHILDREN, AUNTS, UNCLES, COUSINS—WAS GATHERED AT JACK'S PLACE

TO CELEBRATE THE HOLIDAY. JUST AS THEY WERE ABOUT TO SIT DOWN AT THE TABLE, AS MOTHERS WERE HELPING THE CHILDREN FIND THEIR PLACES AND OLDER WOMEN WERE CARRYING FOOD TO THE SIDEBOARD, A CAR DROVE UP. THE CHILDREN, LIKE BIRDS IN FLIGHT, RAN TO THE DOOR TO SEE WHO ELSE HAD COME TO THE FEAST.

JACK SHOOED THEM BACK TO THE TABLE AND OPENED THE DOOR HIMSELF. STANDING ON THE PORCH, JUST OUTSIDE THE SCREEN DOOR, WAS A GOOD-LOOKING MAN WITH NORDIC BLUE EYES AND A CORN-YELLOW MUSTACHE THAT ALMOST COVERED HIS SENSITIVE MOUTH.

"IDA LOUISE," JACK SAID, HIS VOICE FALTERING A BIT, "YOU'D BETTER COME HERE."

SHE BRUSHED PAST HIM IN A FLASH AND WAS THROUGH THE SCREEN DOOR BEFORE HE COULD OPEN IT FOR HER, TEARS STREAMING DOWN HER FACE, AND SHE SAID, "I WOKE THIS MORNING KNOWING YOU WOULD COME HOME TODAY."

ROB TOOK HER GENTLY INTO HIS ARMS AS THOUGH SHE WERE THE CHILD, AND THE LOOK HE GAVE HIS FATHER WAS AS STEADY AND LOVING AS THE ONE JACK WAS GIVING HIM.

"MOM, YOU AND DAD SIT DOWN," HE SAID. HE HELPED HIS MOTHER TO HER CHAIR. "WAIT!" HE SAID, "I'VE SOMETHING TO SHOW YOU." ALMOST IMMEDIATELY HE WAS BACK AGAIN. HE PUT HIS ARM ABOUT A YOUNG WOMAN AND INTRODUCED HER TO HIS PARENTS. "THIS IS MY LOVING WIFE, EMILY, AND YOUNG JACK, OUR SON, WHO IS SOME ATHLETE." THEN HIS DAUGHTER, A SMALL GIRL OF PERHAPS EIGHT YEARS OF AGE, SIDLED UP TO HIM AND SMILED AT HER GRANDMOTHER. ROB BENT DOWN AND KISSED THE CHILD. "IDA LOUISE WANTS TO BE AN ARTIST. SHE GIVES US GREAT JOY."

HE THEN WENT TO HIS FATHER, HUGGED HIM, AND SAID, "DAD, I OWE YOU AN EXPLANATION. FOR MANY YEARS NOW I'VE TAUGHT MUSIC IN SEVERAL HIGH SCHOOLS IN CALIFORNIA, WHERE EMILY AND I HAVE MADE A LIFE FOR OURSELVES AND THE CHILDREN. EMILY IS A VOLUNTEER IN THE SCHOOL SYSTEM. SHE DOES GREAT THINGS FOR

REMEDIAL READERS AND FOR OTHER CHILDREN WHO NEED HER SPECIAL BRAND OF MAGIC."

IDA LOUISE BEGAN TO CRY, AND ROB KISSED HER. "MOM, I PROMISE IT WILL NEVER BE THIS LONG AGAIN. WE HAVE SUMMER LEAVE, AND WE WILL COME BACK NEXT YEAR DURING THE SUMMER, SO OUR CHILDREN CAN PLAY HERE AND BECOME A PART OF THE FAMILY." COUSINS AND AUNTIES AND UNCLES DREW CLOSE AND EVERYONE SHARED TEARS AND KISSES AND WORDS OF WELCOME.

ROB AND HIS BROTHER HELD EACH OTHER CLOSE, AND QUIETLY YOU COULD HEAR THEM SAYING THE WORDS THAT NEEDED TO BE SAID, PROMISING THE PROMISES THAT NO LONGER WOULD BE BROKEN.

A SONG IS HEARD

Out of his heart comes a simple lay,
of Mother's love and trials great,
of innocence lost in fire and blood
and youth that seemed to pass away.

Then from his mother's tender breast
came love, and comfort, solace rare,
that eased the pain and freed the flood
of sorrow and of shame.

Come my son, she said to him, forgive
yourself for those who died. Find the man
who went away, the gentle man, who sang of
of simple things, of wildwood nooks, of
love, and children at their play.

JANE WATSON HOPPING

SHADOWS ON THE MIND

*W*hen Floyd, Aunt Clary's friend, grew old, he often came over to visit with her. He would talk to her about the good old days of his childhood and persuade Auntie to tell him stories of her childhood about living in the great woods. Eventually, he'd say, with tears hanging in his eyes, "My mother is gone, but I'll never forget her, the gentle touch of her hands, the long, golden hair, and laughter. She was a kind woman who sang like a nightingale and played the piano and violin as well. She was so patient with me when I insisted on learning to play the fiddle.

"Sometimes it seems like she's walking with me," he'd say. "I can almost hear her telling me again about the need to love one another or lay hate aside, as she often did when she was alive. After I came home from the war, she held me in her arms and talked to me, and walked for hours in the woods with me, listening. No matter how awful it was she didn't flinch. It was her strength that helped me wash away the pain and anger."

Then he'd laugh and tease Aunt Clary a bit. "Clary," he'd say, "why don't we go down to the barn dance this Saturday! If we're too old to dance we can clap our hands to the music and watch the young folk." Then he'd get serious, almost pathetically so, and he'd ask Auntie, "Do you remember when you were young with golden yellow ribbons in your hair and the young bucks nearly got into fistfights over who was going to dance with you next?"

Aunt Clary would laugh. "Those were wonderful youthful times, weren't they!" she'd say. And they would move a little closer to each other and she would listen while he reminisced. Memories, like golden apples dropping from the bough, filled the lonely hollows in their hearts.

As shadows fell, he would take his cane and lantern and shuffle down the dirt road toward home until he was out of sight. Warmed by his companionship, Aunt Clary would slowly get ready for bed. On stiff knees, she would kneel and ask God to hold Floyd in the palm of His hand and comfort him in his loneliness.

Aunt Clary's Old-fashioned Oatmeal Date-Nut Bars

MAKES 36 BARS

Aunt El used to call these bars, enriched with whole wheat flour, honey, and oatmeal, good-for-your-health bars. She'd tell everyone who stopped by to take two, saying, "They'll keep you healthy, happy, and wise."

½ CUP ALL-PURPOSE FLOUR

¾ TEASPOON BAKING POWDER

½ TEASPOON BAKING SODA

½ TEASPOON SALT

2 TEASPOONS CINNAMON

1 TEASPOON NUTMEG

PINCH OF CLOVES (NOT MORE THAN ⅛ TEASPOON)

¾ CUP WHOLE WHEAT FLOUR

½ CUP BUTTER OR MARGARINE, WARMED AT ROOM TEMPERATURE

¾ CUP HONEY, WARMED AT ROOM TEMPERATURE

2 EGGS, LIGHTLY BEATEN

⅓ CUP MILK

1 CUP QUICK-COOKING OATS

1½ CUPS PITTED, CHOPPED DATES

1½ CUPS COARSELY CHOPPED WALNUTS

POWDERED SUGAR TO DUST

Preheat oven to 375°F. Set out and lightly grease a 13x9x2-inch baking pan.

Into a medium bowl sift flour, baking powder, baking soda, salt, cinnamon, nutmeg, and cloves. Stir in the whole wheat flour. Set aside. In a large bowl beat butter with honey until light and fluffy. Add eggs and continue beating. Stir in the milk, then flour mixture just until ingredients are combined. Fold in oats, dates, and walnuts. Turn into prepared pan.

Bake until a toothpick inserted in the center of dough comes out clean, 35 to 40 minutes. Remove from oven. Transfer to wire rack to cool. While still warm dust top lightly with powdered sugar. Let set until warm and pliable, then cut into bars.

Virginia's Easy-to-Make Hamburger Heaven

1 POUND LEAN GROUND BEEF

1 TEASPOON SALT

¼ TEASPOON PEPPER

¼ TEASPOON GRANULATED GARLIC,
    OR GARLIC JUICE

½ POUND AMERICAN CHEESE,
    GRATED

1 SMALL CAN RIPE OLIVES, SLICED

2 CUPS FLAT NOODLES, COOKED IN
    LIGHTLY SALTED WATER AND
    DRAINED

2 CUPS STEWED TOMATOES (ONE
    15- TO 16-OUNCE CAN)

¼ CUP WATER

MAKES ABOUT 6 SERVINGS

In a large, heavy frying pan crumble ground beef; over high heat brown and partially cook meat. Season with salt, pepper, and garlic. Then add remaining ingredients in layers: cheese, olives, noodles, and tomatoes. Rinse out tomato can with ¼ cup cold water and pour over all. Adjust seasoning with salt and pepper if desired. Cover and cook over medium heat for 30 minutes. Serve piping hot with an easy-to-make salad.

Serve store-bought strawberry ice cream for dessert.

From A Good Man

A good man never dies —
In worthy deed and prayer
And helpful hands, and honest eyes,
If smiles or tears be there:
Who lives for you and me —
lives for the world he tries
To help — he lives eternally.
A good man never dies.

JAMES WHITCOMB RILEY

Mothers work hard to provide nourishing meals for their families. Most appreciative of this fast-supper casserole dish are our youngest women, who sometimes work outside the home by day and still have washing and cooking to do at night, in addition to helping children with homework and listening to their woes.

Thanks, Virginia, for sharing.

NOT OF SILVER OR OF GOLD

$\mathcal{E}$very Thanksgiving Day, Uncle Ned, who reached the age of ninety-six years in 1938, had his hair freshly cut and his mustache trimmed. He got himself all dressed up, patted a little bay rum about his ears, and came to dinner. He seldom brought anything with him. He didn't have to. The women made extra pumpkin and mince pies and cooked a little extra meat, brought home-canned peaches and pears—half a dozen jars each— with them to the dinner.

Uncle Ned would actually leave with more fun and love than he had brought. The women dug about in their baskets and boxes to find the several generous boxes they had packed with goodies for the old man to take home with him. Little children squeezed in beside him on the sofa and young boys came by to wish him well and tell him all about the delicious dishes their mothers had made for the feast. Young women kissed and patted him. Old women sat down near him, held his fragile old hand, and talked to him about the old days.

Uncle Ned basked in the attention.

Then, one year, Danny brought his young bride to the family gathering. When she asked him why everyone was paying so much attention to the old man, he told her that Uncle Ned deserved it. Shortly, men, women, and older children began to sidle up to her to tell her how Uncle Ned, a bachelor for years, through hard times had shared his wealth, crops, cattle, and his own labor with every member of the family. Some told her how he had saved their farms by paying up property taxes. Others, with tears in their eyes, recalled his help when doctor bills piled up. Young women told her about the stove or bed he had bought them when they were newly married. Aunt Kate talked on and on about the kindness he had shown her and other older widows.

Uncle Bud always said it was a mark of respect to tell strangers about the goodness of a man like Uncle Ned.

Uncle Ned's Butter an' Honey Biscuits

2 CUPS ALL-PURPOSE FLOUR

2 TEASPOONS BAKING POWDER

½ TEASPOON SALT

¼ CUP BUTTER, PLUS ¼ CUP MORE
    FOR BUTTERING BISCUITS

⅔ CUP MILK

½ CUP HONEY TO SPREAD ON
    BISCUITS

MAKES 12 BISCUITS

Preheat oven to 450°F. Set out a baking sheet.

Into a large bowl sift flour, baking powder, and salt together, twice. Using a pastry blender or two knives, cut ¼ cup butter into the flour until particles the size of peas form. Add milk all at once and stir until flour is thoroughly dampened. Continue to stir until a soft dough follows the spoon around the bowl. Turn onto a lightly floured surface; knead about 30 seconds. Roll ½ inch thick and cut with a 2-inch-diameter floured biscuit cutter.

Bake until well risen and golden brown, 12 to 15 minutes. Remove from oven; split biscuits in halves; spread lower half with butter and upper half with honey. Put halves together and nest in a napkin in a bun warmer, long enough to allow butter-honey flavor to permeate biscuits. Serve piping hot.

Uncle Ned milked a string of Jersey and Holstein cows. Every day a truck came out from the cheese factory to pick up his metal cans of whole milk and separated cream. He also kept hives of bees for pollinating his orchard and for producing honey, which he gave away and sold.

In the late fall, when folks had a little time on their hands, people held one potluck supper after another. Uncle Ned always brought fresh butter and honey.

BLESS THIS DAY

Dear God, again I'm up just before dawn,
again in time to see your morning promise,
bright and pink, out my kitchen window.
My kids are still sleeping. I'll wake them soon
to get them up for school. I hear my husband
in the shower, and still feel the memory
of the warmth of him holding me
through all of last night.
Soon he will sit beside me,
at our kitchen table,
and we'll talk, just the two of us,
before the kids,
in not much more than whispers,
about our coming day.
Then, I'll give him that old lunch pail
and kiss, and hug him out the door.
At noon he'll find my surprise,
a note wrapped around the extra piece of pie
that says, "I love you."
Thank you, dear God, for life.
Bless our food. Bless this day.

I come to this noontime,
a break in the day,
with the smell of new tires
on hands I've just washed.
I've spent the morning
mounting new tires
on people's cars

so they will be safe on their way
to see family and friends
and earn their daily bread.
I open the old lunch pail
my Dad carried when he
did the same job in the same store.
Make my hands as true as his, Lord, I pray,
and my heart.
Bless this food.
Bless this day.

ALVIN REISS

The Wonder of It All

O UR GRANDMOTHER ALWAYS THOUGHT THERE WAS A SPECIAL GRACE ABOUT SIMPLE WORKING FOLKS WHO GAVE THE BEST OF THEMSELVES TO THEIR FAMILIES, FRIENDS, NEIGHBORS, AND STRANGERS. THEY WERE MEN AND WOMEN WHOSE GOOD HEARTS AND SKILLED HANDS SEEMED TO CALL SHOWERS OF BLESSINGS DOWN UPON THEMSELVES AND THOSE ABOUT THEM.

WE ALWAYS THOUGHT AUNT CLARY AND UNCLE JOHN WERE BLESSED BY GOD. MOTHER COULD RECALL THEIR EARLY MARRIED YEARS, AND HOW THE FAMILY TEASED THEM BECAUSE THEY ACTED LIKE SWEETHEARTS EVEN AFTER THE CHILDREN CAME. SOME ENVIED THEIR HAPPINESS AND CONTENTMENT. UNCLE JOHN TOLD YOUNG BACHELORS TO GET THEMSELVES A GOOD WOMAN LIKE CLARY, AND HE TOLD YOUNG MARRIED MEN THAT HE AND AUNT CLARY WERE LIKE A WELL-MATCHED TEAM OF HORSES THAT COULD PULL ONE WHALE OF A LOAD AND HAVE ENERGY TO SPARE. HE TOLD THEM TO TREAT THEIR WOMENFOLK WITH RESPECT, LOVE, AND KINDNESS.

AS THEY GOT OLDER, CLARY AND JOHN TALKED TO THE CHILDREN IN THE FAMILY ABOUT THE NEED TO SHARE AND TO HAVE COMPASSION FOR OTHERS. THEY SPOKE ALSO ABOUT THE WORTH OF THE UNION BETWEEN A MAN AND A WOMAN, AND THE WONDER

OF IT ALL. THEY ENCOURAGED YOUNG PARENTS TO LOOK INTO THE EYES OF THEIR CHILDREN, TO LET THE LOVE SHINE THROUGH, TO HUG THEM AND TO TELL THEM OVER AND OVER HOW MUCH THEY WERE WANTED AND VALUED.

BUT PERHAPS THE GREATEST LEGACY THEY LEFT ALL OF US WHEN THEY PASSED ON WAS THE SKILL THEY DEMONSTRATED IN BUILDING A LONG-LASTING, STABLE MARRIAGE. MANY OF US HAVE BENEFITED BY FOLLOWING THEIR EXAMPLE.

THE TIES THAT BIND US HEART TO HEART

*W*hen Sheila and I were children, Mother often talked to us about "the ties that bind," about family solidarity. She told us family stories about loving and "looking out" for each other. We were taught that if we wanted to get the most out of our lives we had to share ourselves with our loved ones and with others.

She talked often about her childhood and about Grandpa, who took time to live as well as to make a living. She would laugh and tell stories about his playfulness with her and her brothers and sisters. She told us in detail about homemade baseball diamonds and great swings that hung in the trees. Some of her best stories were about when company came for a harvest supper, after which there would be singing and dancing and games to play.

"Mother," she would say, "was warm and kind. Everyone loved Jenny." Women would go walking in the woods with her and then sit a bit to share life's joys and sorrows. She never complained about cooking for neighbors and friends. "Your grandmother," Mama would tell us, "understood that we are all God's children, that our choice to believe in a higher power gives us strength to build a good life on, one that grows out of a compassionate heart."

Chicken à la King with Homemade Buttermilk Biscuit Braid

MAKES 4 TO 6 SERVINGS

In the thirties this dish was thought to be quite fancy. Effie made it, Aunt Sue made it, and Mother made it for Floyd and Aunt Clary. They served it on hot buttermilk biscuits instead of toast. Effie usually served it on a biscuit braid for pre-Thanksgiving gatherings.

COOKED DICED CHICKEN (RECIPE FOLLOWS)

HOMEMADE BUTTERMILK BISCUIT BRAID (RECIPE FOLLOWS)

½ POUND MUSHROOMS, SLICED

4 TABLESPOONS BUTTER OR MARGARINE

1 GREEN PEPPER, MINCED

1 SWEET RED PEPPER, MINCED

2 TABLESPOONS ALL-PURPOSE FLOUR

1 CUP MILK

1 CUP LIGHT CREAM (HALF AND HALF WILL DO NICELY)

1 TEASPOON SALT

½ TEASPOON BLACK PEPPER

SPRIGS OF PARSLEY, FOR GARNISH (WHOLE OR MINCED)

While Biscuit Braid is baking, in a heavy skillet sauté mushrooms in butter 3 to 5 minutes; add green and red peppers. Cook gently about 5 minutes or more. Add flour and stir until well blended. Slowly add milk and cream. Bring to a boil and stir until smooth and slightly thickened. Reduce heat; add chicken, salt, and pepper, and heat through. Spoon into the center of the Biscuit Braid, garnish with parsley, and serve at once.

Homemade Buttermilk Biscuit Braid

MAKES 1 BRAID

2 CUPS ALL-PURPOSE FLOUR

1½ TEASPOONS BAKING POWDER

½ TEASPOON BAKING SODA

1 TEASPOON SALT

⅓ CUP COLD BUTTER OR MARGARINE

¾ CUP BUTTERMILK

¼ CUP MILK OR THIN CREAM FOR BRUSHING TOP OF BRAID

Preheat oven to 450°F. Lightly grease a large baking sheet.

Into a medium bowl sift flour with baking powder, baking soda, and salt. With a pastry cutter or two knives, cut butter into flour until mixture resembles coarse cornmeal. Make a well in the center of the dry ingredients and add buttermilk all at once. Stir with a fork until dough becomes cohesive, then gently form it into a ball and place on a lightly floured surface; knead about 10 times.

Roll out dough into a rectangle roughly 4x12 inches and about ½ inch thick. Handle as little as possible. With a knife, cut dough lengthwise into three long strips. Carefully braid the strips, pinching them together tightly on each end. Pick braid up cradled in the hands and lay on the prepared baking sheet. Shape the braid into a circle and lightly brush with milk. Bake until golden brown, 15 to 20 minutes.

Cooked Diced Chicken

ONE 3-POUND CHICKEN (A LARGE FRYING CHICKEN WILL DO NICELY)

1 TEASPOON SALT

¼ TEASPOON BLACK PEPPER

½ TEASPOON PULVERIZED DRIED THYME

Wash chicken and remove fat. Into a large saucepan place chicken and giblets. Cover with water; add salt, pepper, and thyme. Bring to a boil. Turn down heat and simmer until meat is fork tender, 45 minutes to 1 hour.

Transfer chicken from saucepan to platter. Reserve the broth. While chicken is still warm discard skin and any remaining fat. Take the meat off the bones; dice breast and thigh meat. Set 2 cups aside. Combine broth and meat that remains on the carcass. Reserve for making soup.

Note: If you do not want to use immediately, freeze in cartons for later use.

Herb Buttered Green Beans

MAKES ABOUT 6
SERVINGS

Hanna raised and canned quarts of Kentucky Wonder string beans. She would sit by the hour, pulling off the strings and snapping them in preparation for canning. When she cooked them fresh in summer, she would snip bits off her herbs to add to them; in fall or winter she used her home-canned beans and dried herbs.

2 POUNDS FRESH GREEN BEANS
    (ABOUT 6 CUPS COOKED)
1 TEASPOON SALT
⅛ TEASPOON BLACK PEPPER
¼ CUP BUTTER OR MARGARINE
1 TEASPOON LEMON JUICE,
    STRAINED

¼ CUP DICED CELERY
3 TABLESPOONS PARSLEY
¼ TEASPOON ROSEMARY
¼ CUP MINCED FRESH CHIVES OR
    WINTER ONIONS (DRY ONIONS
    MAY BE USED)

Wash whole beans, then remove ends and strings. Cut or snap crisp, slender pods into 2-inch pieces. Turn into a large saucepan. Add salt and pepper. Cook in 1 inch boiling water until tender-done, about 15 to 20 minutes.

Meanwhile, melt butter in a small saucepan; add lemon juice, celery, parsley, rosemary, and chives or onions. Sauté 3 minutes, or until chives or onions are tender-done. When beans are done, strain and toss with butter-herb mixture. Serve piping hot.

One Crust Apple Pie

MAKES ONE 9-INCH PIE

This quick-to-make apple pie is one that a young cook or women who work long hours can make in a flash. I sometimes bake the crust during the evening hours, then

FLAKY SINGLE CRUST PASTRY
    (PAGE 101)
3 OR 4 LARGE APPLES (JONATHAN
    PREFERRED), PEELED, CORED,
    AND SLICED
½ CUP SUGAR
1 TEASPOON CINNAMON

½ TEASPOON NUTMEG
2 TABLESPOONS QUICK SMALL-
    GRAIN TAPIOCA
2 TABLESPOONS BRANDY
    FLAVORING
1 CUP SPICED WHIPPED CREAM
    (PAGE 97)

Preheat oven to 425°F. Set out a 9-inch pie pan.

Make pastry, roll out, and line bottom and sides of pie pan. Using a fork, prick holes in dough. Bake until pastry is light and golden brown, 15 to 20 minutes. Remove from oven and set aside to cool.

    While pastry bakes, in a medium saucepan bring apples and ¼ cup water (more if needed) to a boil; immediately turn down heat. Simmer with sugar, cinnamon, and nutmeg. Add tapioca and stir frequently until filling has thickened. Remove from heat; cool to lukewarm or cold as desired.

    Just before serving, blend in brandy flavoring; let the filling set at room temperature. Prepare Spiced Whipped Cream. To assemble, turn apples into the prebaked crust and spread them evenly about with the back of a spoon or a spatula. To serve, spread whipped cream over the filling.

on the following day I cook the apples and assemble the pie just before serving it.

From THE SONG OF HIAWATHA

Ye who love a nation's legends,
Love the ballads of a people,
That like voices from afar off
Call to us to pause and listen,
Speak in tones so plain and childlike,
Scarcely can the ear distinguish
Whether they are sung or spoken; —
Listen to this Indian Legend,
To this Song of Hiawatha!
Ye whose hearts are fresh and simple,
Who have faith in God and Nature,

Who believe, that in all ages
Every human heart is human,
That in even savage bosoms
There are longings, yearnings, strivings
For the good they comprehend not,
That the feeble hands and helpless,
Groping blindly in the darkness,
Touch God's right hand in that darkness
And are lifted up and strengthened; —
Listen to this simple story,
To this Song of Hiawatha!

HENRY WADSWORTH LONGFELLOW

In the Green and Silent Valley Dwelt the Singer Nawadaha; There He Sang of Hiawatha

An avid reader of poetry and fairy stories, Aunt Clary's daughter Martha fell in love with Henry Wadsworth Longfellow's poem *The Song of Hiawatha*, which was based on stories told by several North American Indian tribes. The Indians believed that a miracle created this strong and handsome warrior and that he had come to open up their rivers, show them the way through the forests, and plant for them Indian corn, or maize.

THE GIFT OF MAIZE

*Y*oung Martha was one of the brightest children in the family, and there was little that she did not find fascinating. She haunted the library and listened intently to older family members as they talked about the earth and its bounty.

When she was older and married and had children of her own, she taught them about the richness of life, about simple things that they would not learn about in school, like God's gift of corn.

From the library she learned that the ancient languages, such as Hebrew, Sanskrit, Greek, and Latin, had no words for corn, which now bears the species name *Zea mays* (thus *maize*). Corn was thought to have been developed at least sixty thousand years ago, quite possibly in Mexico, by inhabitants of the Americas. By the time early explorers and settlers arrived on the continent all of the main types of corn grown today were being grown by American natives.

In settlement after settlement, white men learned from the Indians how to plant corn, which through difficult times and hard winters staved off hunger and even starvation. The early colonists used corn instead of money. People paid their rent, taxes, or debts in corn and even traded it for marriage licenses. Looking back, one can hardly overestimate the Indian's gift of maize.

Young Martha's Spoon Bread

1 QUART MILK	1¾ TEASPOONS SALT	MAKES **6 TO 8**
1 CUP YELLOW CORNMEAL, FINELY	4 EGGS, WELL BEATEN	SERVINGS
GROUND	1 TEASPOON BAKING POWDER	
¼ CUP BUTTER OR MARGARINE,		*Martha's family loved*
PLUS SOME FOR TOP		*this old-time bread*

and served it often

Preheat oven to 425°F. Set out and thoroughly grease a 1½-quart casserole.

Scald milk in a double boiler, then gradually stir in cornmeal. Cook to consistency of mush. Add butter and salt. Gradually stir in eggs and baking powder. Pour mush into prepared casserole.

Bake until well risen and top is lightly browned, 45 minutes. Serve hot, topped with butter.

with ham and eggs or
sausages.

Young Martha's Indian Corn Pudding

**MAKES 4 TO 6
SERVINGS**

*Each year Aunt Clary
reminded us that
corn, now grown in
huge fields, was once
a sacred gift, a symbol
of plenty in a time of
want. Young Martha
brought corn dishes
like this vintage corn
pudding to the
Thanksgiving feast
and set it at the
center of the table in
memory of Indians
who taught colonists
to plant corn, thus
handing them the key
to survival.*

5 CUPS MILK
⅓ CUP CORNMEAL
½ CUP HONEY

1 TEASPOON SALT
1 TEASPOON GINGER
½ CUP OR MORE HEAVY CREAM

Preheat oven to 325°F. Thoroughly butter a medium pudding dish. Set aside.

In the top of a double boiler cook milk and cornmeal together for 20 minutes; add honey, salt, and ginger. Pour into prepared dish and bake 2 hours or until a knife inserted in the top comes out clean, not milky. Spoon heavy cream over the top and serve lukewarm.

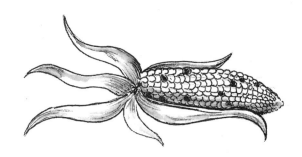

Old-Fashioned Hominy au Gratin

MAKES 6 SERVINGS

*On cold, rainy
evenings in late fall,
Martha often served
hominy baked in a*

1 TABLESPOON BUTTER OR
    MARGARINE
1 TABLESPOON ALL-PURPOSE
    FLOUR
1 CUP MILK
½ CUP GRATED SWISS CHEESE

½ TEASPOON PAPRIKA
1 TEASPOON SALT
2 CUPS COOKED HOMINY
    (1-POUND CAN)
¼ CUP BUTTERED BREAD CRUMBS,
    MORE IF YOU WISH

Preheat oven to 375°F. Set out and thoroughly grease a 1½-quart casserole dish.

Make a sauce of butter, flour, and milk (follow the method for Medium White Sauce on page 10). Add cheese, paprika, and salt. Turn hominy into prepared casserole. Pour sauce over it and cover with bread crumbs. Bake until sauce bubbles and crumbs are lightly browned, 20 minutes. Serve immediately as a main dish or as a side dish with thin slices of leftover ham.

cheese sauce as a main dish. She surrounded it with home-canned snap beans and cabbage and carrot salad, and ended the hearty meal with a light dessert.

OLD-FASHIONED COOKED HOMINY

In the old days hominy was made at home from corn; the whole kernels were soaked in lye water to remove the outer coating of the grain of corn. The kernels were soaked and washed until the tender hominy was free of lye and safe to eat.

Today both yellow and white hominy may be purchased in one-pound cans from most grocery stores. Hominy, popular again, is served with meats, game, and vegetables.

THANK YOU

A happy little thought,
Like a joyous little bird,
Flitted through my mind today
And chased a cloud of gloom away
As in and out it whirred.

I tried to lay ahold of it,
To learn from whence it flew.
And when at last I captured it
And had its secret, every bit
I found it came from you.

LOWELL FILLMORE
Best Loved Unity Poems

Kith and Kin and Kissin' Cousins

PERHAPS THE MOST ENJOYABLE THING ABOUT THE ANNUAL GATHERING OF THE CLAN FOR THANKSGIVING IS GETTING ACQUAINTED AGAIN WITH THE LITTLE ONES—SHARING WITH THEM A COOKIE OR CRACKER PARTY AND SOME OF THEIR LISPING CONVERSATION JUST BEFORE NAPTIME. HOW PLEASURABLE IT IS TO HOLD IN MY HAND, UNTIL THEY WILT, THE SHORT-STEMMED FLOWERS THE LITTLE ONES HAVE PICKED OUT OF THE WEEDS FOR ME ALONE.

ONCE TWO LITTLE SISTERS, ONE FAIR WITH SUNLIGHT IN HER SMILE, THE OTHER SWEET OF FACE WITH SOFT, CURLING, LIGHT BROWN HAIR ENRICHED WITH RED-GOLD HIGHLIGHTS, ARGUED OVER A TIGHT FIST OF COOKIES. THEIR SOFT-SPOKEN FATHER TOLD THEM, "WE DON'T TAKE THINGS FROM OTHER PEOPLE, EVEN OUR SISTERS. WE ASK THEM TO SHARE WITH US. IF THEY DON'T WANT TO, THEY DON'T HAVE TO. JUST BECAUSE WE ASK PEOPLE FOR SOMETHING, IT DOESN'T MEAN THEY HAVE TO GIVE IT TO US."

FROM THE SIDELINES, LOOKING A BIT LEFT OUT OF EVERYTHING, LITTLE COUSINS ABOUT FIVE TO EIGHT YEARS OF AGE WATCHED THE FRAY. THEY WERE REMEMBERING, PERHAPS, THOSE DAYS WHEN EVERY MEMBER OF THE FAMILY SHOWERED THEM WITH HUGS, KISSES, AND LITTLE GIFTS.

JANE WATSON HOPPING

UNCLE BUD, SENSING PERHAPS HOW THEY WERE FEELING, PULLED THE BOYS INTO CONVERSATIONS ABOUT KITES AND CATCH, PETS AND SCHOOL. AUNT SUE TALKED TO THE GIRLS ABOUT COOKING AND SEWING, MUSIC LESSONS, TEACHERS, AND BEST FRIENDS. OLD AUNT FANNY PATTED AND STRAIGHTENED THE GIRLS' HAIR AND RIBBONS AND TOLD THEM IN HER SQUEAKY OLD VOICE THAT SHE LOVED THEM ALL. SOFTLY, YET LOUD ENOUGH TO BE HEARD, EFFIE TOLD THE OTHER WOMEN THAT WE WERE SO LUCKY TO HAVE SUCH NICE GIRLS IN THE FAMILY.

ABOUT THAT TIME, THE IN-BETWEEN CHILDREN BEGAN TO MOVE OUTSIDE FOR ROUGHER PLAY. RICK BEGAN TO BEG THEIR UNCLES TO COME OUTSIDE AND WATCH THEM PLAY. SOON THE MEN MOVED OUT ONTO THE PORCH TO WATCH UNINHIBITED CHILDREN RUN AND JUMP FENCES, THROW SOFTBALLS AND HARDBALLS, WRESTLE ON THE GRASS, AND WHOOP AND YELL UNTIL THEIR FACES FLAMED RED. SEEING THE COLOR RISE IN THEIR FACES, UNCLE NED TOLD US THAT WAS A SIGN OF GOOD HEALTH.

SHORTLY AFTERWARD, AUNT CLARY CALLED ALL OF THE CHILDREN IN TO WASH THEIR HANDS AND FACES AND COMB THEIR HAIR AND SENT THEM TO TAKE THEIR PLACES AT THE THANKSGIVING TABLE. AS THEY RETURNED, PARENTS AND RELATIVES HUGGED THEM AND TOLD THEM HOW SPRUCED UP THEY LOOKED. AUNTIES WHISPERED "I LOVE YOU" INTO THE EARS OF THE GIRLS, PATTED OLDER BOYS ON THE SHOULDER, AND KISSED LITTLE BOYS ON THE CHEEK. UNCLES AND GRANDFATHERS HUGGED THE GIRLS AND KIDDED THE YOUNG MEN AND OLDER BOYS.

UNCLE NED TOLD THE WOMEN, "IN THESE CHILDREN LIES THE FAMILYS' WEALTH!"

WHEN AN OLD MAN GETS TO THINKING

When an old man gets to thinking of the years he's traveled through,
He hears again the laughter of the little ones he knew.
He isn't counting money, and he isn't planning schemes;
He's at home with friendly people in the shadow of his dreams.

When he's lived through all life's trials and his sun is in the west,
When he's tasted all life's pleasures and he knows which ones are best,
Then his mind is stored with riches, not of silver and of gold,
But of happy smiling faces and the joys he couldn't hold.

Could we see what he is seeing as he's dreaming in his chair,
We should find no scene of struggle in the distance over there.
As he counts his memory treasures, we should see some shady lane
Where's he walking with his sweetheart, young and arm in arm again.

JANE   WATSON   HOPPING

We should meet with friendly people, simple, tender folk and kind,
That had once been glad to love him. In his dreaming we should find
All the many little beauties that enrich the lives of men
That the eyes of youth scarce notice and the poets seldom pen.

Age will tell you that the memory is the treasure-house of man.
Gold and fleeting fame may vanish, but life's riches never can;
For the little home of laughter and the voice of every friend
And the joys of real contentment linger with us to the end.

EDGAR A. GUEST

THE GIFT OF OLD-TIME VALUES

*A*unt Clary grew up in a home where morals and values were taught through parables, anecdotes, admonitions, bursts of gentle wisdom, spiritual training, and stern discipline, and by the example of loved adults.

She recalls her father telling her as a child that given a calm, positive nature, one that expected good to come to her, she could expect to live a long, active, productive life. She would tell children that she and her brothers and sisters learned early about perseverance and would say, "We were all taught to stand firm in the face of adversity, not to hide from reality nor turn our backs on problems that had to be dealt with. And we were told that a lot of complaining was a sign of weakness."

Aunt Clary believed that life was too short for one to spend one's energy in fault-finding, revenge, prejudice, and intolerance. She told us that such attitudes and actions were contrary to God's will, and admonished us not to waste our time on such things.

As she got older, some of the fire left her, and from her more gentle side she began to tell us, one after another, that she had tried to live her life so that when she flew away, the lives of those she left behind would be enriched, not hurt or destroyed, by any thought, word, or deed of hers.

Sinful Ginger Beer

MAKES 16 QUARTS OR 32 PINTS

4 GALLONS WATER
6 CUPS SUGAR
6 OUNCES POWDERED GINGER

¼ CAKE COMPRESSED YEAST
6 LARGE LEMONS, SLICED AND SEEDS REMOVED

Aunt Clary was a faithful member of the Young Women's Christian Temperance Union. Since she loved her small grandson Ted, who came to stay with her sometimes for months at a time, she would not let him drink ginger beer or root beer or any kind of old demon rum. She told him, "It is sinful to drink beverages called beer, and no boy of mine will be corrupted by such a habit in this house." It was Uncle Ned who reminded her that ginger beer was not an alcoholic drink and that men and women in the family had made it for generations.

In a large kettle boil water; add sugar and ginger and stir until sugar is dissolved. Cool to lukewarm, then add yeast. Put lemons into a large crock. Pour water-sugar mixture over them and stir to blend. Let the mixture stand for 24 hours. Strain and bottle liquid. Cork securely but not so tightly that the bottles would burst before the corks popped out. (Soda-water bottles or beer bottles should be used, as they are made to withstand pressure.) Store the bottles on their sides in a cool place. Will be ready to drink in 2 to 4 weeks. Serve ice cold.

TRUE FRIENDS

Friendship is a sacred thing,
When it comes with you to dwell,
Be very careful with it,
And guard its beauties well.

It doesn't come to us every day,
In these wide walks of life,
Where every day has its troubles,
And we're burdened with care and strife.

Sunshine friends are many,
But they flit away on wings,
When we are depressed and burdened,
By the cares that trouble brings.

The only true friends we have,
Are those who stand the test,
So be very gracious with them,
For by them we are doubly blessed.

GLADYS MEEKINS WATSON
(MOTHER)

AN OLD-TIME FRIEND

$\mathcal{M}$other once had a dear friend named Veta who had grown up in the hills of Kentucky. She was a simple, quiet woman, not well educated but calm and serious, always dressed in clean, faded cotton. Throughout the summer and into the late fall, she would walk a mile or more to our house, carrying her young son most of the way. Mama always looked forward to seeing her. Mother would tell us that Veta is the kind of friend you can count on, one that knows when to give advice and when to listen.

One Indian summer day, knowing that Daddy and Grandpa would be coming home late, Mother and I decided that we would try to finish cutting up the firewood that they left. We were working hard, using a crosscut saw, when Veta walked in with Gerald. Immediately, she set me to watching her little boy and she took up the other end of the crosscut saw. To Mama she said, "I'll side ya, Gladys."

All that afternoon the women worked. They would stop now and then to chat awhile or drink lemonade. About midafternoon Mother spread an old quilt under the shade of a tree and Veta put her son down to nap. I sat on the quilt for more than an hour playing paper dolls or reading from a library book as I watched the little one sleep.

About four o'clock the women wiped the saws, put them away, carried some of the wood across the yard, and stacked it on the back porch. Mother gave Veta a flour sack of fresh vegetables to take home with her. They gathered up Gerald, the quilt, and lemonade glasses. They lingered at their goodbyes.

On Indian summer days, I frequently think about that long-ago day in October when I first understood what strong cords bind loving friends.

Mother's Favorite Sugar Cookie

MAKES 6 TO 8 DOZEN, DEPENDING ON SIZE OF COOKIE CUTTER

Mama said she first learned to make these cookies from her mother when she was only eight years old. Throughout her lifetime she developed many variations for this basic recipe, all of which have been popular with the family.

1 CUP BUTTER OR MARGARINE, SOFTENED AT ROOM TEMPERATURE
1½ CUPS SUGAR
2 EGGS, BEATEN TO A FROTH
2 TEASPOONS VANILLA EXTRACT
1 TEASPOON LEMON EXTRACT
2 TABLESPOONS MILK OR CREAM
3 CUPS FLOUR, PLUS ½ CUP MORE AS NEEDED TO MAKE DOUGH EASY TO HANDLE
2 TEASPOONS BAKING POWDER
1 TEASPOON SALT

Preheat oven to 375°F. Lightly grease a large cookie sheet.

In a large bowl beat butter or margarine until light. Gradually add sugar, a small amount at a time. Add eggs and stir until blended. In a cup combine vanilla and lemon extract with milk or cream, then add to butter mixture. Stir until incorporated.

In a medium bowl sift flour with baking powder and salt, then add to butter mixture. Beat or stir until well blended. Turn dough out onto a lightly floured surface and shape into a ball (dough should be firm enough to handle). Wash and thoroughly dry bowl. Return dough to clean bowl, cover, and refrigerate until well chilled, 1 hour or more. (Chilled dough rolls more easily and is less likely to stick to floured surface.)

Lightly flour a smooth surface and the rolling pin. Use only as much flour as is necessary for rolling. *Too much flour makes cookies dry and less tender.*

When dough is thoroughly chilled, remove from refrigerator. Roll out ⅓ of the dough into a sheet ⅛ inch thick. Dip cookie cutter in flour and cut out cookies. Lift cut-out cookies with a spatula and lay them on prepared baking sheet, leaving 1½ inches between cookies. Dip cutter in flour often to prevent sticking.

Repeat with remaining ⅔ dough until all dough has been used. Bake until cookies are well risen, light golden brown, and medium firm to the touch, 10 to 12 minutes. Cookies will crisp up as they cool. Store in an airtight container or double wrap in freezer bags and store in the freezer for two to four months.

Sugar Syrup

---

2 CUPS GRANULATED SUGAR   **2 CUPS WATER**   **MAKES ABOUT 2 CUPS**

Combine sugar and water in a 2-quart saucepan, stirring until sugar is dissolved. Place over heat, stirring continually until liquid comes to a boil. Cover. Boil 5 minutes without stirring. Remove from heat. Cool. Store in the refrigerator in a covered glass jar. Use as needed to sweeten juice or iced tea.

Mother preferred to sweeten cold drinks with sugar syrup instead of granulated sugar, which tends to be gritty.

Easy-to-Make Lemonade

---

1 CUP LEMON JUICE, STRAINED   **ICE CUBES OR CRUSHED ICE**   **MAKES 8 SERVINGS**
1 CUP SUGAR SYRUP   **SPRIGS OF LEMON MINT FOR**
8 CUPS COLD WATER   **GARNISH**

In a large container combine lemon juice and syrup and stir until syrup is dissolved. Add cold water; stir to blend. Serve over ice and garnish with lemon mint.

When I was a little girl, iced tea and lemonade were popular soft drinks. Mother had a lovely, light, frosted-green pitcher and eight matching glasses, which she brought out only for serving iced tea or lemonade. We children thought they were very elegant.

HARVEST HOME SUPPER

*A*unt Alice used to tell us stories about her childhood in England and a feast called Harvest Home that was celebrated in the late fall. She would recall with delight the excitement of the rural people as they cut the last of the corn and grain, piling it in carts that were decorated for the occasion with green branches, flowers, and ribbons.

The trip to the barn was wildly festive as field-workers walked beside the carts cheering, laughing, and ringing bells. Young folks rollicked about, sang silly songs, and threw water on the queen of the festival to ensure bounteous rain for the coming year's crops. The barn was something to be seen—garlands were hung everywhere and great tables were set. If the harvest had been especially good there might be numerous serving platters of roast beef, fresh and cured pork hams, and plum pudding. After everyone had stuffed themselves, they began to sing all of the old harvest songs, including songs of praise for God's bounty as well as some rowdy ditties. This was followed by dancing and wild games.

At this point Aunt Alice said she was put to bed, but she did not sleep, and would stay up and listen to the music and laughter well into the night.

Mother's Moist Roast Beef with Carrots, Potatoes, and Brown Gravy

MAKES 6 TO 8 SERVINGS, PLUS ENOUGH LEFTOVER ROAST FOR SANDWICHES OR MEAT PIE

In the late thirties, Mother bought a fancy stainless steel roast pan that had

5-POUND ROAST, CUT FROM THE RUMP, CHUCK, OR ROUND

BUTTER OR MARGARINE TO RUB OVER THE ROAST

3 TEASPOONS SALT

1½ TEASPOONS BLACK PEPPER

1 TABLESPOON DRIED MARJORAM OR OREGANO LEAVES, PULVERIZED

1 CUP OR MORE WATER OR BEEF STOCK

1 WHOLE CLOVE GARLIC, PEELED

6 MEDIUM CARROTS, PEELED AND LEFT WHOLE

5 MEDIUM POTATOES, PEELED AND HALVED

2 LARGE ONIONS, PEELED AND QUARTERED

1 TABLESPOON MINCED PARSLEY FOR GARNISHING

BROWN GRAVY (RECIPE FOLLOWS)

Preheat oven to 350°F. Trim excess fat off meat, then rub just enough butter or margarine over the roast to coat it lightly. Salt and pepper and rub the marjoram over the top. Place in a roasting pan that has a tight cover. Pour 1 cup water or beef stock around the base; add the garlic and roast, covered, until a meat thermometer registers medium-done (155° to 160°F). Then add carrots, potatoes, and onions. Add water if necessary and continue cooking until the vegetables are done. Remove from the oven, put the meat on a large platter, and slice. Surround the roast with the cooked vegetables and sprinkle parsley over all. Pass Brown Gravy separately. Serve piping hot.

vents that opened and closed to regulate steam and allowed the meat to be basted easily. Each year, when the harvest celebrations began, she would pull it out of her cupboard and use it to fix meals for family and friends, that were fit for a king.

Brown Gravy

2–3 CUPS WATER OR BEEF STOCK   5 TABLESPOONS CORNSTARCH   MAKES ABOUT 3 CUPS

As soon as the meat has been removed, spoon floating fat off the liquid left in the pan; add enough water or stock to pan liquor to make 3 cups. Bring to a boil (see note). Moisten cornstarch in cold water and stir into boiling broth all at once, continuing to stir until the gravy is clear and thickened.

    Note: To give the gravy a rich color, put 1 tablespoon granulated sugar into a small cast-iron skillet; turn on the heat and stir occasionally until sugar has melted and become bubbly and dark brown. Add ¼ cup boiling water (take care as it bubbles up). Pour into boiling broth before thickening the gravy.

Granny Smith Apple Slaw

MAKES 6 SERVINGS

This slaw, made from fruit stored in the apple house and the basement, has always been one of Mother's favorite fall and wintertime salads. She served it often with fresh pork and ham.

In her later years, when she discovered Granny Smith apples in the stores, she used them almost exclusively in this salad.

3 CUPS (ABOUT ¾ POUND) SHREDDED CABBAGE

3 CUPS CRISP APPLES, WASHED, PARED, CORED, AND FINELY CHOPPED (GRANNY SMITH PREFERRED)

3 TABLESPOONS MINCED PARSLEY

2 TEASPOONS MINCED CHIVES

DRESSING

¼ CUP LEMON JUICE

½ CUP LIGHT CREAM OR HALF AND HALF

2 TABLESPOONS SUGAR

1 TEASPOON SALT

PINCH OF BLACK OR WHITE PEPPER (LESS THAN ⅛ TEASPOON)

In a medium bowl combine cabbage, apples, minced parsley, and chives. In a small bowl stir together lemon juice, thin cream, sugar, salt, and pepper. Pour dressing over all and toss to coat vegetables.

Leave the salad in the bowl in which it was made or transfer it to a decorative bowl for passing at the table. If you wish, cover salad plates with lettuce, spoon the salad onto plates, and serve individually.

IN THY PRESENCE WE ABIDE

Our Heavenly Father
We thank You for ministering to us,
for fellowship,
for this gift of food
to nourish our bodies.

We pray Your blessing
upon our guests

and ask You to guide them
safely on their journeys
as they travel to and fro
and ask You to guide us
as we go out
into Your beautiful world.

Amen

ALVIN REISS
—AFTER A GRACE BY REV. ROBERT GRISWOLD,
RETIRED EPISCOPAL PRIEST,
LAKEVIEW, OREGON, SENIOR CENTER,
NOV. 6, 1991

Whole Wheat Buttermilk Rolls

2 TABLESPOONS (PACKAGES) GRANULATED YEAST

¾ CUP WARM WATER (105 TO 115°F)

1½ CUPS ALL-PURPOSE FLOUR, PLUS ½ CUP FOR KNEADING

3 CUPS WHOLE WHEAT FLOUR

2 TABLESPOONS SUGAR

2 TEASPOONS BAKING POWDER

2 TEASPOONS SALT

¼ CUP BUTTER OR MARGARINE, MELTED, THEN COOLED, PLUS 2 TO 3 TABLESPOONS SOFTENED AT ROOM TEMPERATURE FOR BRUSHING TOPS OF ROLLS

1¼ CUPS BUTTERMILK

MAKES 1 DOZEN

These simple-to-make rolls require only one rising. Women and girls in our family often take them to pre-Thanksgiving reunions, private parties, and harvest suppers, and to family gatherings for Thanksgiving Day dinners.

In a small bowl soften yeast in warm water; set aside. Thoroughly grease 13x9x2-inch pan.

Into a large bowl sift 1½ cups all-purpose flour with 1 cup whole wheat flour, sugar, baking powder, and salt. Make a well in the center of the dry ingredients. Stir the cooled, melted butter into buttermilk. Pour liquid ingredients into well of flour; stir until a soft, thick batter is formed. Gradually add remaining 2 cups whole wheat flour; stir into a soft, slightly sticky dough. Turn out onto a well-floured surface; roll into a rectangle the size of the pan. Place in pan. With a sharp knife score dough 1 inch deep to make 12 rolls. Brush the tops with 1 or 2 tablespoons softened butter. Let rise in a warm place until double in bulk, 45 minutes to 1 hour.

Meanwhile, preheat oven to 425°F. Bake rolls until well risen, evenly browned, and firm to the touch, 20 to 25 minutes. When done remove from oven and serve piping hot.

Sheila's Pan Fried Parsnips

MAKES 6 OR MORE SERVINGS

12 TENDER YOUNG PARSNIPS (OR 6 LARGE PARSNIPS)
SALT AND PEPPER TO TASTE

⅔ CUP FLOUR OR FINE BREAD CRUMBS, MORE AS NEEDED
½ CUP OR LESS COOKING OIL

By Thanksgiving spring-planted parsnips are about as big as a small to medium carrot. The following spring, they will have grown huge yet will still be sweet and good flavored. Either size parsnip will do for this recipe.

Scrape parsnips and boil until tender. Drain. When cold, cut them into long, thin quarters. Season each quarter lightly with salt and pepper. Dip each slice in flour or bread crumbs and sauté in oil until both sides are golden brown. Drain on brown paper. Serve piping hot.

HIGH PRAISE

Our fathers paused and set one day apart
To thank Thee, gracious Lord, for food to
eat.
I too would thank Thee from my inmost
heart
For the harvest yield. But oh, I find it sweet
To pause today, remembering the things
Throughout the year that gave my spirit
wings.

No less than gifts of corn and wheat and rye,
No less than this Thy gift, my sheltering
roof,
Are the elusive things: the star-drenched sky,

High winds, the sun, blue distance, crags
aloof,
Unreachable, yet beckoning me to climb
Higher than earth through limitless space
and time!

I do not need a dim cathedral's light,
An organ's rolling thunder as I pray.
I want a hill, wind-swept and clean and
bright,
Where I can reach and thank Thee, Lord,
today
For a thousand things so often we pass by
Without a prayerful word or lifted cry.

GRACE NOLL CROWELL
Best Loved Unity Poems

Ada's Pear Custard Pie

SINGLE CRUST PASTRY PLUS
(PAGE 12)
¼ CUP FLOUR
1 CUP LIGHT BROWN SUGAR,
FIRMLY PACKED
3 RIPE BOSC OR D'ANJOU PEARS,
PEELED, HALVED, AND CORED

1 EGG, BEATEN TO A FROTH
1½ CUPS MILK
¼ TEASPOON LEMON EXTRACT
½ TEASPOON GROUND CINNAMON

MAKES ONE 9-INCH PIE

Bosc pears are large, yellow or greenish yellow in color, and covered with brown rust, which is part of their natural coloring. These fall pears are good keepers, juicy and delicious when ripe, perfect for desserts. To ripen, put in a paper bag and set out at room temperature.

Preheat oven to 450°F. Make pastry, roll out, and cover bottom and sides of a 9-inch pie tin with it. In a small bowl thoroughly blend 2 tablespoons of the flour with ¼ cup of the sugar; sprinkle evenly over the bottom of the pie shell. Arrange pear halves, core side up, in the pie shell. In a medium bowl blend egg and milk with lemon extract; pour over the pears. In a second small bowl blend remaining flour with remaining sugar and the cinnamon. Sprinkle over pear halves.

Bake for 10 minutes, then reduce oven setting to 325°F and bake 30 minutes more or until custard is firm and a knife blade inserted into it comes out clean.

D'Anjou pears are large and creamy yellow green. When they ripen they're excellent for both desserts and canning. These winter pears are also good keepers and quite flavorful when ripe.

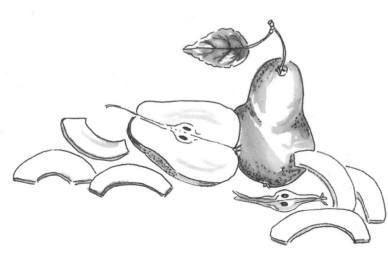

A Star in the Night, or a Pillar of Fire

Shortly after graduating from high school, Aunt Mabel left Missouri to teach in a backwoods school in Oklahoma. She always said that her Little Red School House years were the source of her most fondly remembered experiences. She believed that there are important things that children should be taught, things that should become a part of their lives. Most particularly, she insisted that we know about "this wonderful country of ours." She told us stories about great men like Abraham Lincoln and George Washington, and about women like Florence Nightingale. And she reminded us that civilization is always built by men and women of vision, values, and creativity.

JANE WATSON HOPPING

OF SUN AND RAIN

Was a lovely but cool day, some sun and partly
cloudy. Had a great rain through midnight.

I need to do cakes and some art work
for the bazaar next week. I'm enjoying the
wood stove. It gets so cold in the living room.
Mary brought me a cactus in bloom
and a fresh trout for taking care of her
little dog, who came along and raced with mine.

That trout was so delicious.
Wish you could have some.
Rain due in tonight.

OPAL GUETZLAFF

A GATHERING OF THE SHEAVES

$\mathscr{A}$s Thanksgiving approaches, Aunt Esther tells us again about the gathering in of the sheaves. She tells how neighbors assembled each year in one home or another, on Saturday evening before Thanksgiving Day, all knowing that the upcoming event would be more than a party.

She vividly remembers neighbors in cars, wagons, or buggies pulling into their farmyard around dusk. Those already gathered early would dash out to greet those who had just arrived. They helped old folks and younger women and girls out of their vehicles, carrying babies, small children, tall cakes, trays of cookies and pies. Some folks stayed outside and chatted in the crisp fall air. Men laughed loudly, shook hands, and patted each other on the back. Women hugged each other and the older children. Boys and girls gathered in knots, excited to be together again.

As it got frostier, everyone went inside. The house was filled to the brim. Guests set out on a large table the cookies, cakes, and pies they had brought. Smaller tables were set up and filled in almost every room. Aunt Esther's mother and several other women made a big pot of coffee and several pots of tea.

Shortly, one could hear men talking about the best potato crop they'd ever had, about foals, cattle prices, about a son that had bought himself a place or a daughter who had made someone a grandfather for the first time.

Women talked about sons and fathers who had built them a new front room, about grandchildren who had spent the summer with them and older family members who were feeling better.

Aunt Esther says she can still hear all the shared blessings. "Ain't that nice?" a woman in a faded dress would say to her neighbor, or "You deserve it, Ellie," and "I'm so glad for you, dear."

Later when the cakes, cookies, and pies had been demolished, and the coffeepot and teapots emptied, the young women with small children started gathering up their belongings, and everyone began to tell each other how wonderful it was to hear all the good news. Someone would remark that it just lifted the heart and made a person even more grateful than they had been when they arrived. How good it was to feel that the neighborhood was strong and stood solidly together in good times as well as bad.

In time, hugs and kisses, backslapping, and hearty laughter sent first this one and then that on their way home.

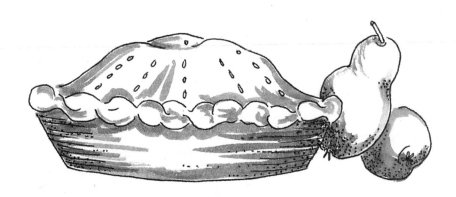

From GOD BLESS YOU EVERYONE

Though we say in parting
Goodby, farewell to you,
That parting word is more a prayer;
It's really "God bless you."

CARL FRANGKISER
Best Loved Unity Poems

Ada's Wiener Schnitzel

6 VEAL CHOPS OR STEAKS

SALT AND PEPPER TO TASTE

2 EGGS, BEATEN TO A FROTH

FLOUR AS NEEDED FOR DIPPING,
   PLUS 1 TABLESPOON FOR
   THICKENING

3 TABLESPOONS BACON DRIPPINGS

JUICE OF 1 LEMON

1 CUP THICK SOUR CREAM

1 LEMON CUT CROSSWISE INTO
   THIN SLICES

MAKES 6 SERVINGS

Ada's friend Johanna shared this recipe with our family. It was a dish we were not too familiar with, but it soon became a family favorite.

Set out a large, heavy skillet.

Sprinkle veal with salt and pepper. Dip into egg, then into flour. Brown on both sides in hot bacon drippings. Cover and cook slowly over medium heat until chops are tender, about 1 hour. Sprinkle with lemon juice and arrange on a hot platter. Blend 1 tablespoon flour with fat in the pan; add sour cream and cook 3 minutes, stirring constantly. Adjust seasoning as you wish and serve with chops; garnish with lemon slices, and Old-Fashioned Mashed Potatoes (page 175).

Spinach Salad with Lemon French Dressing

**MAKES 6 TO 8
SERVINGS**

*Our family loves this
late-fall salad. With
rain, summer spinach
still left in the garden
sends tender leaves
well above the
ground. Even
Grandpa, who
usually did not like to
try new things, took a
fancy to this simple
salad.*

2 POUNDS TENDER YOUNG
    SPINACH, CAREFULLY WASHED
½ POUND MUSHROOMS, THINLY
    SLICED
1 MEDIUM SWEET RED ONION,
    PEELED AND THINLY SLICED

2 HARD-COOKED EGGS
LEMON FRENCH DRESSING
    (RECIPE FOLLOWS)

Use only thick, tender spinach leaves for salad (save larger, tougher leaves for cooking). Shake excess water off leaves. Into a large bowl, tear spinach leaves into small pieces. Add sliced mushrooms and onion; fold together. Chop egg whites and yolk separately. Gently add to the salad. Moisten with Lemon French Dressing.

Lemon French Dressing

MAKES 1 CUP DRESSING

½ CUP LEMON JUICE
½ CUP VEGETABLE OIL
1 TEASPOON SALT
1 TEASPOON PAPRIKA

2 TABLESPOONS HONEY
½ TEASPOON CELERY SEED
1 SMALL CLOVE GARLIC, MINCED

In a wide-mouth jar combine ingredients in the order listed. Shake well, then refrigerate. Before serving, shake a second time.

Al's Favorite Pecan Cookies

2 CUPS ALL-PURPOSE FLOUR

1½ TEASPOONS BAKING POWDER

¼ TEASPOON SALT

½ CUP BUTTER OR MARGARINE,
   SOFTENED AT ROOM
   TEMPERATURE

1 CUP SUGAR

1 EGG, SEPARATED

1 CUP PECANS, FINELY CHOPPED

¼ CUP CINNAMON SUGAR
   (INCLUDING 1 TABLESPOON
   OR MORE CINNAMON)

MAKES 6 DOZEN
COOKIES

Preheat oven to 375°F. Set out a large cookie sheet.

Into a medium bowl sift flour with baking powder and salt; sift again. In a large bowl cream butter thoroughly. Gradually add sugar; cream together until light. Beat egg yolk well and add egg yolk and flour mixture to butter-sugar mixture. Stir to blend. Fold in nutmeats. Chill. When firm enough to handle, roll into balls the size of large marbles (size and number of cookies will depend on size of hand-rolled balls). Place dough balls on cookie sheet and press flat with tines of a fork. Brush tops with lightly beaten egg white and sprinkle with cinnamon sugar.

Bake until cookies have risen and are lightly browned and firm to touch, 10 minutes. Remove from oven. Transfer to wire rack or brown paper to cool. When thoroughly cooled, store in an airtight container or put about a dozen or more at a time in plastic freezer bags and fasten top securely. *Note:* Cookies will keep for two or more months in freezer.

WITH LOVE

I think with love the whole day long,
I work with love the whole day through;
It quickens joy in me and adds
Importance to the things I do.

R. H. GRENVILLE
Best Loved Unity Poems

Like other country women, Ida Louise loved Sand Tarts; even so, she argued that the cookies would be even more delicious if finely chopped pecans were included in the dough, as opposed to the traditional practice of garnishing the tops of the cookies with three halves of split almonds.

Effie, always self-confident and independent, urged Ida Louise to "go ahead and make up a batch to suit yourself." And so encouraged, she did, and called them Ida Louise's Delicious Pecan Cookies. Even though years have passed we still make them, and share them with friends like Alvin Reiss.

PRICELESS GIFTS

*A*unt Lula Hopping's rich beautiful voice is so melodious that when she sings old-fashioned hymns like "The Old Rugged Cross," "In the Garden," "Amazing Grace," and others before the congregation on Sunday morning, even the hardest heart softens, and tears fill the most skeptical eyes.

When she coaxes us to pray along with her, one has the feeling that God is near and that Lula is speaking to a beloved Father. The words pour forth softly as she asks him to shower our lives with blessings and to give us strength and wisdom.

She's a loving mother, grandmother, and great-grandmother. Her home is warm and comfortable, and feels lived in. Throughout her life hungry young 'uns have known they were welcome to fill up on her delicious chocolaty Jelly Roll Cake. She still tells us that, though many years have passed, her life is filled with excitement and happiness. She mentions how her family is blessed with the love of children, most recently by the birth of twin great-granddaughters—born four minutes apart—who are so sweet and lovely that the sight of them makes her heart sing.

Aunt Lula's Jelly Roll Cake

1 CUP (2 STICKS) MARGARINE

4 TABLESPOONS COCOA

1 CUP WATER

2 CUPS SUGAR

2 CUPS FLOUR

2 EGGS, LIGHTLY BEATEN

1 TEASPOON BAKING SODA

1 TEASPOON VANILLA

½ CUP BUTTERMILK

SERVES A BUNCH OF

HUNGRY BOYS

Boys who are now men graying at the temples still fondly recall days when Lula welcomed them with Jelly Roll Cake and games around the kitchen table. Some mist up as they reminisce about her kindness and gentle mothering.

Preheat oven to 400°F. Set out and grease a 15x10x1-inch jelly roll pan.

In a small saucepan bring margarine, cocoa, and water to a boil. In a large bowl blend sugar and flour together. Pour hot margarine-cocoa mixture over flour-sugar mixture and stir together. Add eggs, baking soda, vanilla, and buttermilk. Blend well. Pour into pan.

Bake until well risen, browned, and springy-firm to the touch, around 20 minutes. Remove from oven and frost while hot with Vanilla Nut Frosting. Cool on a wire rack.

Vanilla Nut Frosting

⅓ CUP MILK

½ CUP (1 STICK) MARGARINE

1 POUND POWDERED SUGAR

1 TEASPOON VANILLA

1 CUP CHOPPED NUTS (OPTIONAL)

MAKES 1 OR MORE

CUPS

In a medium saucepan bring milk and margarine to a boil. Remove from heat. Add powdered sugar and vanilla; beat until well blended. Spread while warm over hot cake. Sprinkle top with nuts if desired.

HOARY-FACED PUMPKINS

HOBGOBLIN NIGHT

Silver cornstalk villages
marching row on row
call out Autumn's coming
then Winter and the snow.

Hoary-faced pumpkins
squat stodgily outside
While families of field mice
gather cozily inside.

Soon the children will be coming
from the schoolhouse round the bend
To pick their special pumpkin
before Hobgoblins descend.

PATRICIA PARISH KUHN

*B*y the end of October, Mother Nature is preparing for winter. During this transition, myriads of insects are killed by the frost, most birds have migrated south, farmers are busy bringing in the harvest and storing crops for winter. Among these crops are all of the great squashes and pumpkins that farmers put in warm storerooms that will preserve them well beyond Christmas into the new year.

Late apples harvested at the end of October overflow in apple houses. Soon they will be retrieved for making pies and celebrating Halloween. Shortly, children, like their grandparents before them, will disguise themselves with masks and costumes and go from door to door crying out, "Trick or treat!" Sometimes they give a spooky performance in return for treats.

Colleen's Favorite Pumpkin Bars

1 CUP BUTTER OR MARGARINE,
SOFTENED AT ROOM
TEMPERATURE

2 CUPS SUGAR

2 EGGS, LIGHTLY BEATEN

2 CUPS (ONE 16-OUNCE CAN)
PUMPKIN

2 TEASPOONS BRANDY EXTRACT

4½ CUPS ALL-PURPOSE FLOUR

2 TEASPOONS BAKING POWDER

2 TEASPOONS BAKING SODA

1 TEASPOON SALT

1½ TABLESPOONS CINNAMON

1 TEASPOON NUTMEG

1 TEASPOON GINGER

PINCH CLOVES (LESS THAN ⅛
TEASPOON)

2 CUPS CHOPPED NUTMEATS
(PECANS OR WALNUTS
PREFERRED)

2 CUPS DARK RAISINS

BRANDY FLAVORED GLAZE (RECIPE
FOLLOWS)

MAKES ABOUT
6 DOZEN BARS

One rainy mid-October day well before Thanksgiving, Colleen and I decided to make pumpkin bars. Since we didn't have a recipe we made one up, tested it, and changed it until we knew it was going to be perfect for a mother-and-daughter holiday cooking spree!

Preheat oven to 350°F. Set out and thoroughly grease two 15½x10½x1-inch baking sheets.

In a large bowl cream butter and sugar together until light. Add eggs, pumpkin, and brandy extract. In a medium bowl sift flour with baking powder, baking soda, salt, and spices. Turn flour mixture, all at once, into the pumpkin mixture. Stir until a soft dough is formed. Fold in nuts and raisins. Divide dough in half; spoon dough equally into each of the two prepared baking sheets. With floured hand pat layer of dough over bottom of the first prepared baking sheet; do the same with remaining dough over bottom of second sheet.

Bake until well risen, firm to the touch, and light brown around the edges, 18 to 20 minutes. Remove from oven. Cool about 5 to 8 minutes. Meanwhile, prepare Brandy Flavored Glaze. While bars are still warm, spread them with the glaze.

Brandy Flavored Glaze

MAKES ABOUT 1 CUP

1½ CUPS POWDERED SUGAR

3 TABLESPOONS BUTTER OR
MARGARINE, SOFTENED AT
ROOM TEMPERATURE

1 TABLESPOON MILK OR LIGHT
CREAM, MORE IF NEEDED

1 TEASPOON BRANDY EXTRACT

In a small bowl blend sugar, butter, and combined milk and extract. Beat to a light, spreadable consistency.

Ada's Honeyboys

MAKES 2½ TO 3 DOZEN

Ada named her cookies after the little boys in her neighborhood. All the young ones knew this, but only her own sons knew that there was no honey in Honeyboys.

1½ CUPS ALL-PURPOSE FLOUR

1 TEASPOON BAKING POWDER

½ TEASPOON SALT

½ CUP BUTTER OR MARGARINE,
SOFTENED AT ROOM
TEMPERATURE

½ CUP GRANULATED SUGAR

2 EGGS, SEPARATED

1 TEASPOON VANILLA

1 CUP LIGHT BROWN SUGAR

1 CUP FINELY CHOPPED WALNUTS

Preheat oven to 350°F. Set out and lightly grease a cookie sheet.

Into a medium bowl sift flour with baking powder and salt; sift a second time; set aside. In a large bowl cream butter or margarine; add granulated sugar and beaten egg yolks. Blend well. Add vanilla and flour a little at a time to form a stiff dough.

Turn the dough out onto a lightly floured surface, then pat into ½-inch thickness on cookie sheet. Press down with a fork. Beat egg whites until stiff; add brown sugar gradually. Fold in nutmeats. Spread evenly over dough.

Bake until risen, brown, and done throughout, 20 minutes. Don't overbake! Remove from oven, let set for 10 to 15 minutes, then cut into bars.

November Chill, Chrysanthemums, Boys, and Football

WHEN RANDY WAS IN THE SIXTH GRADE HE PLAYED ON THE GRIFFIN CREEK SCHOOL FOOTBALL TEAM. HE HAD ALREADY TAKEN PART IN PARADES AND BICYCLE RACES, BUT THE LONG-AWAITED FOOTBALL GAME ON THANKSGIVING AFTERNOON HAD HIM IN A DITHER.

RAYMOND AND I WENT DOWN TO THE NEARBY SCHOOL TO WATCH THE GAME AND TO CHEER OUR HOMETOWN BOYS TO VICTORY. NOT BEING FOOTBALL FANS, WE HELD HANDS AND FOLLOWED RANDY'S PLAYS ALL THROUGH THE GAME. I MUST ADMIT THAT THIS MOTHER WINCED EVERY TIME HE WAS TACKLED AND EVERY TIME HE KICKED OR MISSED THE BALL.

AFTER THE GAME, WE TOOK HIM AND SOME OF HIS TEAMMATES OUT FOR PIZZA. THE YEARS HAVE PASSED, AND I DON'T REMEMBER WHETHER THE GRIFFIN CREEK BEAVERS WON OR LOST. I VIVIDLY REMEMBER, THOUGH, THE LOOK ON OUR SON'S FLUSHED FACE AND ON THE FACES OF THE YOUNG BOYS THAT CLUSTERED AROUND US. ALL THROUGH THE INTERVENING YEARS, I HAVE KNOWN THAT ON THAT AUSPICIOUS DAY, ON A GREEN PLAYING FIELD, OUR SON STEPPED THROUGH A THRESHOLD, ONE THROUGH WHICH HE WILL NEVER RETURN.

HOMETOWN HEROES

There is something special about little boys and football. If they have a good coach, young warriors learn self-discipline, fair play, and the value of practice. They learn the value of team effort, camaraderie, self-evaluation, and coordination, all of which comes to full play in manhood.

From A Dream of Autumn

Fields of ragged stubble, wrangled
With rank weeds, and shocks of tangled
Corn, with crests like rent plumes dangled
Over Harvest's battle-plain;
And the sudden whir and whistle
Of the quail that, like a missile,
Whizzes over thorn and thistle,
And, a missile, drops again.

James Whitcomb Riley

Yellow Tomato Preserves

10 LARGE YELLOW TOMATOES, WASHED AND CORED
1 CUP SUGAR
1½ CUPS HONEY (CLOVER HONEY PREFERRED)

JUICE OF 2 LEMONS, STRAINED
1 TEASPOON GROUND CINNAMON
¼ TEASPOON GROUND GINGER
¼ TEASPOON GROUND CLOVES

MAKES 5 TO 6 HALF-PINTS

Aunt Sue made these preserves in the late summer every year. They had many uses and were especially good as a glaze on one of the smoked hams Uncle Bud cured and hung in his smokehouse.

In a large, heavy saucepan, cook unpeeled tomatoes until tender-done. Drain off the waterlike juices; puree the solid meat. Measure and return 6 cups of puree to the saucepan. Add sugar, honey, lemon juice, cinnamon, ginger, and cloves. Cook over medium heat until the puree is thick. Turn off heat and ladle tomato butter, while still hot, into scrubbed, sterilized half-pint canning jars; wipe off the tops of the jars with a clean cloth and seal with sterilized lids and rings. Put the jars into a boiling water bath; bring the hot water to a slow bubbling boil and cook for 15 minutes. Then carefully remove jars from the kettle. Set them on a towel out of cold drafts and let cool. Before storing in a cool, dry, dark cupboard, test the seal: The center of the lid should be concave and when tapped with a spoon should have a hollow sound.

Aunt Mabel's Processed Baked Ham

MAKES 15 TO 20 SERVINGS

10- TO 12-POUND PROCESSED HAM (MAY BE PURCHASED AT ANY GROCERY STORE)

YELLOW TOMATO PRESERVES (PAGE 157) WHOLE CLOVES, AS NEEDED

When the family lived in Missouri, baked ham meant one that was smoked and cured, then boiled in a large pot of water to reduce salt content and render out fat. Uncle Bud, who was known for his curing and smoking skills, set aside some of his hams for family use—get-togethers, harvest home feasts, and pre-Thanksgiving suppers. And in his own quiet way he shared his hams with young and old alike who, through no fault of their own, found themselves in hard straits.

Preheat oven to 300°F. Set out a shallow baking pan that has a rack, and lay out a large brown paper bag that has no printing on it.

Wipe ham with a damp cloth, then wrap loosely in the brown paper bag (don't cover meat tightly enough to steam it; don't add water). Place wrapped ham fat side up on the rack in the baking pan.

If you are using a thermometer, bake until internal temperature reads 150°F. (Or allow 15 minutes per pound for hams that are 12 pounds and over; for smaller hams, 22 minutes.) About 30 minutes before the ham will be done, remove brown paper and cut off the rind. Trim off excess fat, leaving only ¼ inch. Make a series of shallow gashes across the fat so that it is marked with diamonds or squares. Cover the ham with glaze and insert a clove into each square of fat.

Bake uncovered at 325°F until glaze has a nice color, about 30 minutes more.

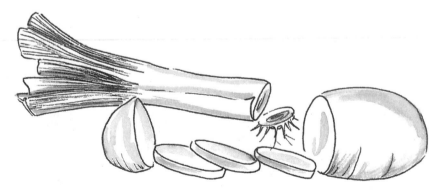

Our Favorite Carrot Salad with Sour Cream Dressing

2 CUPS GRATED CARROTS, WELL
    PACKED
1 LARGE SWEET APPLE, PEELED,
    CORED, AND CHOPPED
    (GOLDEN DELICIOUS
    PREFERRED)

½ CUP DARK RAISINS
½ TEASPOON SALT
DUSTING OF BLACK PEPPER (LESS
    THAN ⅛ TEASPOON)
SOUR CREAM DRESSING (RECIPE
    FOLLOWS)

MAKES 4 TO 6
SERVINGS

Carrots are a real standby in winter, since they keep well in storage or in the ground, where they can be dug anytime there is a thaw. All of our animals, especially horses and rabbits, love them and eat them leaves and all.

In a medium bowl combine grated carrots, chopped apple, and raisins. Sprinkle with ½ teaspoon salt and pepper to taste. Remove sour cream dressing from refrigerator and add just enough dressing to carrot mixture to moisten it.

Sour Cream Dressing

2 TABLESPOONS SUGAR
¼ TEASPOON SALT
DASH OF WHITE PEPPER (BLACK
    MAY BE SUBSTITUTED)

2 TABLESPOONS LEMON JUICE
1 CUP SOUR CREAM

In a small bowl, combine ingredients; blend well. Chill until needed.

Grandma's silly squash
huge beyond compare
no doubt will see
the soup pot
before the County Fair.

NO BLUE RIBBON
PATRICIA PARISH KUHN

Grandma's Holiday Winter Squash Pudding

MAKES 8 SERVINGS

Winter squashes keep well and can be used into the spring as vegetables in soups and puddings. This steamed pudding is a family favorite and is often brought to pre-Thanksgiving suppers or other festivities.

2 CUPS ALL-PURPOSE FLOUR, SIFTED

1½ TEASPOONS BAKING POWDER

¼ TEASPOON BAKING SODA

1½ TEASPOONS SALT

½ CUP BUTTER OR MARGARINE, SOFTENED AT ROOM TEMPERATURE

1 CUP DARK BROWN SUGAR, FIRMLY PACKED

¼ CUP LIGHT HONEY (CLOVER PREFERRED)

½ TEASPOON GROUND CINNAMON

½ TEASPOON FRESHLY GRATED NUTMEG

½ TEASPOON GROUND GINGER

¼ TEASPOON GROUND CLOVES

2 EGGS, WELL BEATEN

1 CUP WINTER SQUASH, COOKED AND PUREED

½ CUP SOUR CREAM

1 CUP WALNUTS, CHOPPED

Thoroughly grease a 2-quart mold and set aside.

Into a medium bowl sift flour with baking powder, baking soda, and salt. In a large bowl cream butter, brown sugar, honey, cinnamon, nutmeg, ginger, and cloves until light. Add eggs and beat until thoroughly blended. Add flour mixture alternately with squash and sour cream to butter mixture, beginning and ending with flour mixture. Fold in nuts. Turn into the prepared mold.

Cover the mold. (If it does not have a cover, butter a piece of heavy brown paper and tie it over the top; or tie a piece of buttered muslin over the top, buttered side down.)

Place mold on a rack or trivet in a large kettle. Pour enough boiling water into the kettle so water comes halfway up the side of the mold. Cover the kettle and steam pudding 2 hours. Check occasionally during the cooking time, making sure that the water is still boiling and that its level is halfway up the mold. When done remove from water; let stand 5 minutes; then unmold onto a serving plate.

UNDER THE LACE-COVERED DINING TABLE

Stuffed with Aunty's pun'kin pie
and turkey dressin', too,
country cousins giggled
as sleep came to too few.

Chatty aunts and uncles
gossiped long into the night,
our little ears reddening
but safely out of sight.

"Uncle Harry drinks too much,
in the corncrib late at night."
"Why! cousin Ruby's spendin'
is not within her right!"

"Now children, mind your manners.
You know better 'an to spy
Upon your aunts and uncles, Dears
Now hush and don't you cry."

PATRICIA PARISH KUHN

To Sit Again at the Groaning Family Board

AUNT SUE USED TO SAY, "THERE'S NOTHING LIKE A FAMILY ALL SITTING AROUND A LONG TABLE, HOLDING HANDS AND SINGING 'OLD HUNDRED,' JUST BEFORE THE FOOD IS PASSED AROUND. IF THERE'S ROOM, BABIES SHOULD SIT AT THE TABLE WITH THEIR PARENTS OR GRANDPARENTS, AND OLDER CHILDREN NEED TO SIT AT A TABLE BY THEMSELVES SO THEY CAN ENJOY THEIR FOOD AND CONVERSATION."

UNCLE BUD AGREED WITH HER AND TOOK LITTLE EDWARD UP ON HIS KNEE. AFTER GRACE, UNCLE BUD FED EDWARD A FEW BITES AND THEN ENCOURAGED HIM TO EAT OUT OF HIS OWN BOWL. SOMETIMES AT BIG FEASTS LIKE THANKSGIVING DINNER, THE LITTLE ONES WOULD ARGUE AND CRY OVER WHOSE LAP THEY WOULD GET TO SET ON. FORTUNATELY, THERE WERE ENOUGH ADULTS IN THE CROWD TO SQUEEZE, HUG, PET, AND HELP FEED ALL OF THE BABIES AND TODDLERS.

BEFORE EATING THEIR OWN MEAL, YOUNG MARTHA AND THE OTHER YOUNG WOMEN HOVERED OVER AUNT CLARY, FLOYD, UNCLE HENRY, AND THE REST OF THE OLD FOLKS, SEEING THAT THEY HAD PLENTY, THAT THEY HAD NOT DROPPED THEIR NAPKIN ON THE FLOOR OR SPILLED SOMETHING ON THEIR BEST CHURCH CLOTHES. THE YOUNG FOLK HELPED

ELDERLY FAMILY MEMBERS IN AND OUT OF CHAIRS AND SPREAD THEIR BREAD AND BUTTER FOR THEM, WHILE STILL HAVING PLENTY OF TIME TO SHARE IN THE FEASTING THEMSELVES.

WHEN DINNER WAS OVER, YOUNG GIRLS FROM THE CHILDREN'S TABLE HELPED THE WOMEN GATHER UP THE USED DISHES AND SET OUT DESSERT PLATES. THEIR MOTHERS RINSED AND STACKED ALL OF THE DINNER PLATES. OLDER WOMEN THEN WASHED AND DRIED THE MANY CUPS, SAUCERS, PLATES, SERVING DISHES, AND MORE. AUNT CLARY, WHO FELT LEFT OUT AND WHO NO LONGER MANAGED THE "CLEANUP" CREW, COMPLAINED THAT THE OTHER WOMEN JUST WANTED TO BE ALONE SO THEY COULD TALK ABOUT HER.

LATER, WHEN BABIES WERE PUT DOWN FOR NAPS AND YOUNG CHILDREN RESTED ON OLD QUILTS SPREAD ON THE FLOOR, THE GROWN-UPS SETTLED DOWN TO CHAT. UNCLE HENRY, ALMOST ASLEEP HIMSELF, WOULD SAY, "FOOD AND FAMILY, FAMILY AND FOOD. AIN'T IT GRAND!" AT WHICH POINT CHILDREN WOULD GIGGLE, YOUNG FOLKS WOULD GIVE EACH OTHER A KNOWING GLANCE, AND UNCLE HENRY WOULD DROP OFF TO SLEEP.

HUNTER'S MOON

There's hay in the barns
and silos filled with grain
the cream's in the butter churn
and the wood pile's out of rain.

There's a Hunter's Moon above
wild turkeys in the trees
the menfolk late for supper
chasing wild rabbits probably.

The harvest's been bountiful
the family free from strife
the fire's warm and comforting
Dear God you've blessed our life.

PATRICIA PARISH KUHN

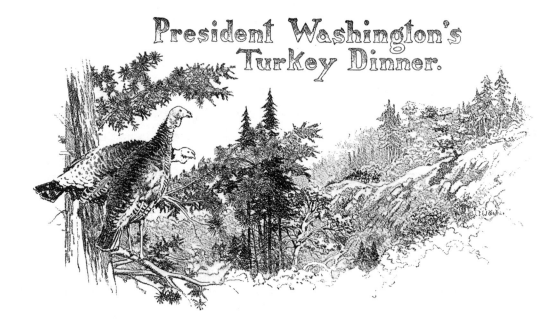

President Washington's Turkey Dinner.

THIS BOUNTY TO AFFORD

*M*other fondly remembers the special Thanksgiving celebrations of her childhood. She recalls that about fifty good neighbors and a gaggle of children would gather in the small community church to thank God for the success of their farming enterprises, the health of their children, and the bounteous blessings of the earth.

After which would come the harvest supper. Women of the church had long since laid plans for the feast; each had a small list of what she would contribute. About one o'clock the tables were set up among the trees and soon ladened with meats, breads, vegetable dishes, homemade pickles and relishes, and mixed fruit salad.

Effie brought a hand-crocheted tablecloth for the table on which tall cakes with whipped frostings were placed, along with pies and tarts, cookies, and small glass plates of fudge and divinity.

Mother laughs when she recalls going home at dusk, carrying with her a napkin filled with goodies.

Turkey with Orange Pecan Dressing and Golden Glow Gravy

ONE 12- TO 14-POUND BIRD

2 OR MORE SHALLOTS AS DESIRED

4 OR MORE WHOLE STALKS OF
CELERY

1 WHOLE CLOVE GARLIC, PEELED

1 TART UNPEELED APPLE
(OPTIONAL)

BUTTER OR MARGARINE AS
NEEDED, SOFTENED AT ROOM
TEMPERATURE

SALT, ALLOWING 1 TEASPOON OR
LESS PER POUND AS DESIRED

BLACK PEPPER, ¼ TEASPOON PER
POUND

1 TABLESPOON OR MORE FINELY
PULVERIZED MEDITERRANEAN
OREGANO

ORANGE PECAN DRESSING
(RECIPE FOLLOWS)

GOLDEN GLOW GRAVY (RECIPE
FOLLOWS)

12 TO 15 SERVINGS
WITH LEFTOVERS FOR
SANDWICHES

In the old days turkeys, related to pheasants, were considered by Indians, colonists, and pioneers to be the noblest game bird in America. It rivaled the bald eagle as a national symbol. Our forests were rich in small flocks of common wild turkeys, which left their cover only long enough to feed on small nuts, seeds, insects, and berries. At night they returned from eating to roost in trees. Hens laid their cream-colored, speckled brown eggs in nests of dry leaves on the ground.

Though not as numerous as they once were, wild turkeys

Preheat oven to 350°F. Set out a large roasting pan with a tight-fitting cover.

Rinse turkey inside and out with cold water. Wipe with a damp cloth. Stuff cavity with shallots, stalks of celery, clove of garlic, and apple. Rub entire surface with butter and then rub salt, pepper, and oregano into it. In a small bowl set giblets (excluding liver) and neck aside; refrigerate for making broth to use in dressing and gravy.

Set bird in roasting pan, breast side up. Pour 2 or more cups of water around the base of the bird. Cover. Roast until done, checking now and then to see if more water is needed, about 2½ hours. To test for doneness insert meat thermometer into densest meat of the inner thigh near the hip bone or groin, since that is the last place to be done in the bird. Be sure not to touch bone with tip of thermometer.

When done, the temperature should read 170°F to 180°F. Or you may test for doneness by pressing the drumstick: When done, the meat will feel soft and the drumstick should twist out of joint; also, the meat will have shrunk up the bone so that the joint where the foot was removed will be bare.

Once done, remove bird from oven and let set 15 to 20

still inhabit the forests of North America. Today's domesticated turkeys are descended from the wild birds of southern Mexico, not those that are hunted in the wilds of the United States and Canada.

minutes, which makes carving easier. Meanwhile, remove giblets and neck from refrigerator and place in a medium saucepan. Season to taste with a little salt and pepper; add a slice or two of winter-cooking onion and ½ cup or more fresh celery leaves. Cover with water and simmer until done; remove meat from pan; discard vegetables; remove neck meat from bone and finely chop all meat (reserve all or part of meat if adding either to dressing or gravy).

Make the dressing and gravy and serve immediately.

Orange Pecan Dressing

At our house we bake dressing in a separate baking dish instead of packing it into the cavity of the turkey. We believe that the unstuffed turkey roasts faster, both inside and out, and that slow-cooking warm stuffing in the bird might result in food poisoning.

8 CUPS TORN PIECES OF BREAD (A BLEND OF WHOLE WHEAT, RYE, AND GOLDEN EGG BREAD IS BEST)

1½ CUPS PECANS, COARSELY CHOPPED, PLUS A DOZEN OR MORE HALVES FOR GARNISHING TOP OF DRESSING

1 CUP CELERY, CHOPPED

¼ CUP FRESH PARSLEY, MINCED

1½ TEASPOONS MEDITERRANEAN OREGANO

GRATED RIND OF A LARGE ORANGE

1½ CUPS BROTH, MORE AS NEEDED (HOT WATER MAY BE SUBSTITUTED)

¼ CUP MELTED BUTTER, PLUS ¼ CUP FIRM BUTTER FOR DOTTING TOP OF DRESSING

SALT AND BLACK PEPPER TO TASTE

Preheat oven to 350°F. Set out and thoroughly grease a 13x9x2-inch baking dish.

In a large bowl combine the torn bits of bread, pecans, celery, parsley, oregano, grated orange rind, broth, ¼ cup melted butter, salt, and pepper. Blend well. Spoon into prepared baking dish. Dot top with remaining ¼ cup butter. Arrange pecan halves on the top of the stuffing.

Prebake until risen, lightly browned, and firm to the touch, about 45 minutes—don't overbake. Rewarm when you bake last-minute rolls such as Mother's Potato Refrigerator Rolls (page 95), or with turkey during the final 45 minutes roasting time.

Golden Glow Gravy

After the turkey is done, take the bird out of the roasting pan and put it on a large platter. Cover it with a clean kitchen towel and let it sit. Put the roasting pan in a cold place until the fat is firm enough to lift off the pan drippings.

Transfer the drippings to a saucepan large enough for making gravy. Add water, salt, and pepper to the drippings to enhance the flavor. Minced giblets and minced neck meat may be added at this point.

While bringing the broth to a boil, caramelize sugar in a small cast-iron frying pan by heating it until it bubbles and turns dark brown (care must be taken not to burn the sugar, which would make it bitter). While still hot, pour the caramelized sugar into the broth. Spoon a little of the broth into the frying pan to wash all of the sugar out.

Stir the gravy until it is a rich golden-brown color. To thicken, add cornstarch (2 tablespoons, moistened with cold water, for each cup broth). Continue stirring for about 5 minutes to sufficiently thicken the gravy. For added flavor, add butter or margarine to the hot gravy. Stir it until it's melted and incorporated into the gravy.

MAKES 1 QUART OR MORE

The women in our family thought food should not only taste good but should look good, too. So in the late thirties they decided to fancy up turkey gravy, which they thought was an unappetizing color.

Aunt Irene's Molded Cranberry Orange Salad

MAKES 6 TO 8 SERVINGS

When Aunt Irene unmolded this brilliantly colored cranberry-orange ring out onto a round glass platter, garnished it with slices of unsweetened pineapple, cream cheese balls, and red maraschino cherries, everyone knew the festivities were about to begin. Children rushed to find their places at the table, men sat down at designated places. Thanksgiving dinner was at hand!

2 CUPS UNCOOKED CRANBERRIES
2 SMALL NAVEL ORANGES
1 CUP SUGAR
1 PACKAGE LEMON GELATIN, SWEETENED OR ARTIFICIALLY SWEETENED
AT LEAST 6 LEAVES LIGHT GREEN LEAF LETTUCE
1 POUND SHRIMP (OPTIONAL)
6 SLICES UNSWEETENED PINEAPPLE
3 OUNCES CREAM CHEESE
1 SMALL JAR MARASCHINO CHERRIES
WHIPPED CREAM MAYONNAISE (RECIPE FOLLOWS)

Set out and oil a 1-quart (4-cup) mold.

Wash cranberries and dry them. Peel oranges; reserve rind from 1 orange. Put whole cranberries and 1 orange peel through a food processor or blender. Turn into a medium bowl. Dice orange pulp; remove seeds. Add orange pulp and sugar to the cranberry mixture. In a small bowl dissolve gelatin in 1 cup boiling water; set aside to cool. Combine liquid gelatin with cranberry-orange mixture, then pour into prepared mold. Chill until firm.

Just before serving, unmold the gelatin onto a bed of lettuce. Fill center with medium-sized pink shrimp, if desired. Arrange pineapple slices around the edges of the molded gelatin; place a round ball of cream cheese in the center of each pineapple slice; add maraschino cherries as a final beautifying touch. With the salad, pass Whipped Cream Mayonnaise.

Whipped Cream Mayonnaise

½ CUP HEAVY CREAM

1 CUP MAYONNAISE

1 TABLESPOON LEMON JUICE,
STRAINED

4 TEASPOONS POWDERED SUGAR

MAKES ABOUT 2 CUPS

Just before serving, whip the cream into soft peaks that will hold their shape. Add mayonnaise, lemon juice, and powdered sugar. Stir to blend, gently, so as not to lose volume.

Ida Louise's Mashed Sweet Potato Caramel

2 CUPS SWEET POTATOES
(LEFTOVER SWEET POTATOES,
EITHER BAKED OR BOILED,
MAY BE USED FOR THIS DISH)

½ CUP OR MORE MILK OR CREAM
SALT AND PEPPER TO TASTE
½ CUP MAPLE SYRUP
¼ CUP BUTTER

MAKES 4 TO 6
SERVINGS

Preheat oven to 400°F. Thoroughly grease an 8x8x2-inch casserole dish.

Thoroughly mash freshly cooked sweet potatoes (or in a medium saucepan heat to lukewarm peeled leftover potatoes, then mash). Add sufficient milk or cream to make a soft texture; season lightly with salt and pepper. Turn into prepared baking dish. Pour thick maple syrup heated with butter over the sweet potatoes. Bake until top is caramelized (watch carefully so it doesn't burn). Remove from oven and let set about 5 to 8 minutes before serving.

Each year, just before Thanksgiving, Ida Louise receives a large tin of 100% pure maple syrup from her cousins in Vermont. The syrup is made entirely from the sap of tall, sturdy sugar maple trees. Every thirty-five gallons of sap, gathered when the ground is blanketed with snow, is "boiled down" until it yields one gallon of medium amber, richly flavored syrup.

Easy-to-Make Thanksgiving Punch

MAKES 12 TO 16 SERVINGS

This punch is a natural beverage choice for a family gathering, and is easy and well liked by all. Effie, who had an apricot tree, canned apricot nectar during the summer months to use for this late-fall drink.

3 CUPS CANNED OR BOTTLED APRICOT JUICE

JUICE OF 3 LARGE OR 4 SMALL ORANGES

2 QUARTS SWEET APPLE CIDER

1 QUART MILD TEA (EARL GREY PREFERRED)

2 DOZEN OR SO RED MARASCHINO CHERRIES

Combine apricot juice, orange juice, cider, and tea. Chill thoroughly. Serve in tall glasses over crushed ice, each garnished with 2 red maraschino cherries.

Effie's Tomato Soup Cake with Cream Cheese Frosting

½ CUP BUTTER OR MARGARINE, SOFTENED AT ROOM TEMPERATURE

1 CUP SUGAR

1 EGG, BEATEN TO A FROTH

1 CAN CONDENSED TOMATO SOUP (UNDILUTED)

1 TEASPOON BAKING SODA

1¾ CUPS ALL-PURPOSE FLOUR, MEASURED AFTER SIFTING

2 TEASPOONS BAKING POWDER

½ TEASPOON SALT

1 TEASPOON GROUND CINNAMON

½ TEASPOON FRESHLY GRATED NUTMEG

1 CUP DATES, FINELY CHOPPED

1 CUP WALNUTS, FINELY CHOPPED

CREAM CHEESE FROSTING (RECIPE FOLLOWS)

MAKES ONE 9x12x2-INCH SHEET CAKE

Thanksgiving at our house would not be the same without someone making this old-fashioned cake. Mama remembers that it was very popular in the thirties and that Aunt Irene had copied Effie's recipe and passed it on to her.

Preheat oven to 325°F. Thoroughly grease a 9x12x2-inch baking pan. Set aside.

In a large bowl cream butter and sugar. Add egg and mix thoroughly. Add soup, in which baking soda has been dissolved, alternately with flour, which has been sifted a second time with salt, cinnamon, and nutmeg. Beat after each addition, then fold in dates and walnuts (if dates are sticky, coat with 1 tablespoon flour).

Turn batter into prepared pan. Bake until well risen, browned, and firm to the touch, about 45 to 50 minutes. When done remove from oven. Cool in the pan.

When thoroughly cool, frost with Cream Cheese Frosting.

Cream Cheese Frosting

3 OUNCES CREAM CHEESE, SOFTENED AT ROOM TEMPERATURE

1 TABLESPOON MILK, SLIGHTLY MORE IF NEEDED

1½ CUPS POWDERED SUGAR, SIFTED IF NECESSARY

½ TEASPOON VANILLA EXTRACT

MAKES ABOUT 1 CUP FROSTING

In a small bowl blend all ingredients until light and of a spreading consistency (adjust amount of milk as needed to obtain a light, smooth-textured frosting).

AN EVENTFUL THANKSGIVING DAY

A woman I once met, named Elisabeth Armstrong, told me that her grandmother had once scared away thieving Indians.

In 1874 her great-grandparents, Nancy and Ben Dawkes, and her grandmother, who was then only four years old, lived on an isolated cattle ranch in northwestern Montana. They were surrounded by a few cattle ranches, and the families running these were as isolated as themselves. There were Indians in those parts and more than enough rough-and-ready scoundrels.

That year, her great-grandfather, after promising her great-grandmother that he would be back before the Thanksgiving pies were out of the oven, left his young wife and child to ride out and check on his cattle. When he did not return by midafternoon Great-grandmother began to worry. She played for a while with the child, then, as darkness came on, she lit all of the kerosene lamps, stoked up the fire, barred the door, and locked the windows.

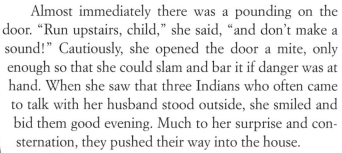

Almost immediately there was a pounding on the door. "Run upstairs, child," she said, "and don't make a sound!" Cautiously, she opened the door a mite, only enough so that she could slam and bar it if danger was at hand. When she saw that three Indians who often came to talk with her husband stood outside, she smiled and bid them good evening. Much to her surprise and consternation, they pushed their way into the house.

"You give food!" they said. "Bread, meat, tobacco!"

"No," Great-grandmother told them firmly, "I have none to spare!"

"You give!" the youngest Indian said, and took her by the arm. "Big Man Ben, he gone!" Afraid for herself and for her child, Great-grandmother did not resist. She prayed that they would take what they wanted and leave.

Then to their astonishment, all of them heard the firm tread of boots overhead in the loft bedroom. The Indians huddled and talked to each other, then as the heavy footfalls began to descend the stairs, the Indians bolted and ran. Great-grandmother quickly barred the door, took the shotgun off the wall, and quietly crept toward the stairs. Softly, she called to her daughter.

"Here I am," piped a small voice. And around the corner of the stairway came the child, a puckish smile on her face, almost swallowed up in her father's boots. "I scared 'em away, didn't I!" she shouted.

And in that moment she became a family heroine, admired for her quick-wittedness and courage by generations to come.

Old-Fashioned Cream of Pumpkin Soup

2 CUPS OR SLIGHTLY MORE PUMPKIN (½ SMALL PIE PUMPKIN)

3 CUPS MILK

3 TABLESPOONS CORNSTARCH

3 TABLESPOONS BUTTER OR MARGARINE

1 CUP LIGHT CREAM

3 TABLESPOONS LIGHT BROWN SUGAR

¼ TEASPOON FRESHLY GRATED NUTMEG

SALT AND PEPPER

MAKES 6 TO 8 SERVINGS

Most of the women in our family have modern-day as well as special old-time Thanksgiving Day recipes. One such traditional favorite is this tasty pumpkin soup made with the sweet, rich-flavored, smooth-textured flesh of baby pie pumpkin.

Cut the pumpkin in half and store one half. With the other half, remove seeds, then pare off skin. Cut pumpkin flesh into 1-inch pieces. Place in a saucepan; pour enough water over to cover, about 1 quart. Simmer until pumpkin is soft and very well done. Strain through a colander, then puree the flesh. Turn strained liquid and puree into a large saucepan. Add 2¾ cups milk and water as needed to the saucepan. Bring to a simmer over medium heat. Meanwhile, combine the reserved ¼ cup milk with cornstarch in a small bowl. When well blended, stir into the pureed mixture. Continue to simmer over low heat for 15 to 20 minutes. Stir occasionally. Blend in the butter, light cream, brown sugar and season with nutmeg, salt, and pepper.

Serve in large, flat soup bowls with whole wheat bread.

Pot Roast of Elk with Pan Gravy

MAKES 12 SERVINGS AND LEFTOVERS

In the days of wood-burning cookstoves, game was often roasted slowly on the back of the stovetop over low heat in large iron pots with tight-fitting lids. Meanwhile, loaves of bread baked inside the oven. This combination filled the whole house with a warm, delicious fragrance.

⅓ CUP OR MORE BUTTER OR
   SHORTENING
5- TO 6-POUND ELK CHUCK, RUMP,
   OR ROUND ROAST
SALT (ALLOW ½ TEASPOON PER
   POUND, MORE IF YOU WISH)
PEPPER (ALLOW ¼ TEASPOON OR
   LESS PER POUND)

1 CUP ALL-PURPOSE FLOUR FOR
   DUSTING MEAT
6 TO 8 LARGE POTATOES
6 TO 8 SMALL ONIONS
6 TO 8 MEDIUM TO LARGE CARROTS
PAN GRAVY (RECIPE FOLLOWS)

Set out a deep, heavy Dutch oven and melt butter or shortening in it. Turn off heat.

Rub the meat with salt and pepper; roll in flour to cover. Reheat fat; brown the roast on all sides. Slip a low rack under the meat to keep it from sticking to the pan. Add ½ cup water; cover the pan tightly. Set the pan over low heat; cook slowly until meat is done, about 3 hours. Add more water as needed.

An hour before the meat is done, pare potatoes, peel onions, and scrape carrots; quarter all vegetables; lay them around the roast and cook until meat is tender and vegetables feel soft when forked. Remove meat from Dutch oven and place on a large platter. Cover lightly with a clean kitchen towel. Make gravy with the pot liquor.

Pan Gravy

3 CUPS THIN PAN DRIPPINGS FROM
   ROASTING ELK (SKIM FAT OFF
   TOP AND ADD ENOUGH WATER
   TO MAKE 3 CUPS)

5 SCANT TABLESPOONS
   CORNSTARCH
¾ CUP WATER, MORE IF NEEDED
SALT AND BLACK PEPPER
BEEF BOUILLON IF DESIRED

MAKES ABOUT 4 CUPS

In a medium saucepan heat pan drippings to a rolling boil. Dissolve the cornstarch in the water, stirring to blend. Stir cornstarch into the boiling drippings and cook just until the gravy becomes clear, about 3 to 5 minutes, stirring occasionally. Remove from heat; season to taste with salt and pepper. Set aside to cool slightly.

Old-Fashioned Mashed Potatoes

6 MEDIUM-LARGE POTATOES
⅔ CUP HOT MILK
⅓ CUP OR MORE BUTTER AS
   DESIRED, PLUS A BIT FOR
   TOPPING THE DISH

SCANT TEASPOON OF SALT
BLACK PEPPER (OPTIONAL)

MAKES 6 SERVINGS

Peel and wash potatoes, put in a large saucepan, cover, and cook in boiling salted water over medium heat until soft. Drain. Shake pan gently over low heat to evaporate water and prevent sticking. Remove from heat. Mash. Add hot milk, ⅓ cup or more butter, salt, and pepper, if desired. Beat until fluffy and white. Serve with a bit of butter on top.

Aunt El taught us girls to boil old potatoes that have been in storage instead of newly harvested ones for mashed potatoes. She thought they beat up much lighter. Effie often added a teaspoon of baking powder to a large pan of mashed potatoes, which whitened and lightened them further.

Quick and Easy Brown Sugar Prune Cake

MAKES ONE 9-INCH SQUARE CAKE

This simple old-fashioned cake is still a late-fall favorite in our family. On cold, blustery days, it is delicious when served with hot coffee, tea, or cold milk.

½ CUP BUTTER OR MARGARINE, SOFTENED AT ROOM TEMPERATURE
1½ CUPS GOLDEN BROWN SUGAR, FIRMLY PACKED
2 EGGS, BEATEN TO A FROTH
½ CUP COOKED, CHOPPED PITTED PRUNES
1½ CUPS ALL-PURPOSE FLOUR
1 TEASPOON BAKING SODA
¼ TEASPOON SALT
1 SCANT TEASPOON CINNAMON
½ TEASPOON FRESHLY GRATED NUTMEG
½ TEASPOON ALLSPICE
PINCH (⅛ TEASPOON) CLOVES
⅔ CUP BUTTERMILK
½ CUP PECANS, FINELY CHOPPED
SWEETENED WHIPPED CREAM (RECIPE FOLLOWS)

Preheat oven to 350°F. Thoroughly grease and flour a 9-inch square baking pan. Set aside.

In a large bowl cream butter and sugar together until light and fluffy. Blend in eggs, then stir in the prunes. Into a medium bowl sift flour with baking soda, salt, and spices. Alternately add flour mixture and buttermilk to the creamed mixture. Fold in the pecans, and pour the batter into the prepared pan.

Bake until a toothpick inserted in the center of the cake comes out clean, about 40 to 50 minutes. Remove from oven and set the pan on a wire rack; cool in the pan to lukewarm. Cut into wedges and serve with a dollop of whipped cream.

Note: Aunt El always made this recipe with cooked prunes, but Aunt Sue often substituted finely chopped dates softened in a little hot water.

Sweetened Whipped Cream

MAKES 2½ CUPS

1 CUP HEAVY CREAM
¼ CUP SUGAR
1 TEASPOON VANILLA

Beat the cream until it is well fluffed and begins to mound. Add the sugar a little at a time, beating after each addition. Add the vanilla and beat a few times to blend. Continue beating as necessary until the cream is glossy. Serve in dollops on desserts.

A Season for Leftovers

Through the years the women in the family have developed recipes for using leftover beef, pork, chicken, and certainly Thanksgiving turkey. When we think the casserole dish, rice dish, or vegetable dish just right we add it to our late-fall or winter list. Included here are some of our favorites.

Easy-to-Make Turkey Squares

3 CUPS CHOPPED LEFTOVER
    TURKEY
2 CUPS WHOLE WHEAT BREAD
    CRUMBS
¼ CUP CHOPPED ONION
½ TEASPOON OREGANO
¼ TEASPOON POWDERED GARLIC
¼ TEASPOON NUTMEG

1 CUP COOKED RICE
⅓ CUP DICED CELERY
4 EGGS, WELL BEATEN
2 CUPS TURKEY BROTH OR
    THINNED GRAVY
1 CAN CREAM OF MUSHROOM SOUP
½ CUP MILK

MAKES 6 OR MORE
SERVINGS

Our young women are all creative cooks. Their recipes are bolder than ours were. They add cream of mushroom soup to this and that dish and use dried onions and herbs that never graced our cupboards. We take great pleasure in tasting their creations, one of which is this recipe that features Thanksgiving leftovers.

Preheat oven to 350°F. Set out and thoroughly grease a 13x9x2-inch baking dish.

In a large bowl combine turkey, bread crumbs, onion, oregano, garlic, nutmeg, rice, celery, eggs, and broth. Turn into large baking dish; distribute evenly in the dish with the back of a spoon. Bake until lightly browned, 45 to 50 minutes.

Meanwhile, to a can of cream of mushroom soup add ½ can of milk. Heat; stir to blend. Cut baked turkey mixture into squares. Serve hot squares topped with heated soup.

A Simple Turkey Pie

**MAKES 6 SERVINGS,
ONE 9- TO 10-INCH PIE**

*After Thanksgiving,
the women in our
family always made
several turkey pies.
They served them
piping hot with the
last of the garden
tomatoes, sliced, and
apples and pears.*

**PASTRY FOR TOP CRUST (RECIPE
FOLLOWS)**

FILLING
3 TABLESPOONS BUTTER OR
MARGARINE
¼ CUP FLOUR
1¼ CUPS BROTH FROM THE ROAST
TURKEY OR THINNED GRAVY
1 CUP MILK
½ TEASPOON SALT
⅛ TEASPOON BLACK PEPPER
¼ TEASPOON POULTRY SEASONING
AS DESIRED
2 CUPS DICED LEFTOVER TURKEY
1 CUP FINELY DICED COOKED
CARROTS
⅔ CUP COOKED PEAS

Preheat oven to 400°F. Set out pie pan. Prepare pastry. Chill until needed.

In a large saucepan melt butter or margarine; blend in flour. Add broth, milk, salt, pepper, and poultry seasoning. Cook, stirring constantly, until filling is thickened. Add turkey, carrots, and peas. Heat thoroughly. Pour filling into pie pan; top with prepared pastry (see directions for crust). Turn pastry edges under and press firmly to the pan. Bake until crust is browned and filling is bubbling, 30 to 35 minutes.

PASTRY FOR TOP CRUST
1 CUP FLOUR
¾ TEASPOON BAKING POWDER
½ TEASPOON SALT
⅓ CUP BUTTER OR MARGARINE
2½ TO 3 TABLESPOONS WATER

Sift flour with baking powder and salt. With pastry cutter or fingertips blend in butter or margarine until flour mixture is crumbly. Add water a little at a time; blend lightly. Dough should be just moist when shaped into a ball. Chill.

When chilled, prepare a lightly floured surface. Roll dough into a ¼-inch-thick circle; shape to fit top of pie pan. Make a few small slits near the center so that steam can escape.

A BREATH AWAY

Raindrops streak the breath-steamed window
of the 12th Street Diner, inches from our faces.
My partner and I face each other
in the wooden booth. We are
in mid-shift, he and I, and our blue-and-white
sits secure at the curb. The radio on my belt
crackles with compact voices.
It is not our call.

If our call should come
in the very midst of our meal,
we will answer, he and I.
With Your help and Your grace, dear Lord,
we will not be wanting.

I chose to be a policewoman, God,
after I felt you touch my life.
I ask Your blessing on myself and my partner
as we travel the city to protect and serve.
And I ask, O Lord, for both our sakes,
that You protect us as we serve You,
and as we serve
the good in society around us.
We are closer than marriage, he and I,
because our lives are in the hands of each other
all the working day,
as both our lives are in Yours.

The waitress, my first-name friend,
sets our lunches before us.

We thank You, Lord,
for her serving hands and heart.
We are serving her, the safety of her family.
We thank you, Lord, for this food.
May it nourish us
to thy work and glory.
Guide us safely through this day
back to the hearts of our families
where we may lay aside our arms
and sleep.
Amen.

ALVIN REISS
© 1991

The Red Skies of Evening

Laura, Ida Louise's eldest daughter, was so much like her grandfather on her mother's side of the family that her father's people were sometimes "put out" because she didn't resemble them in any way. Her hair, almost gold in color, and flashing green eyes bore out her lineage.

Her Uncle Bill loves to tell stories about her, about the day he found her hanging on a limb in a tall fir tree. His most often-told tale is about the day the family looked out the window and saw her standing in the yard, feet firmly planted, back straight, green eyes unblinking, staring down the family's two-thousand-pound bull. Her brothers wanted to run out and chase the bull away, but their father told them to stay inside. He loaded his rifle and stood at the door watching the standoff. In time, the bull backed away. "He knows how he got out, just move slowly and he'll go back in the same way," her father told her.

Laura never moved a muscle until the bull turned away and jumped the fence; then she ran to the house and told her mother, "I'm not going to be scared of that old bull!"

In high school Laura was athletic and always at the top of her class. She excelled in cooking classes, math, and history. Her parents often thought she might teach school or become an accountant. To their surprise she

CAME TO THEM THE DAY AFTER GRADUATING FROM HIGH SCHOOL TO TELL THEM SHE HOPED TO GO INTO LAW ENFORCEMENT. THE FAMILY WAS CONCERNED ABOUT HER BEING INVOLVED IN SUCH DANGEROUS WORK. HER BROTHERS AND MALE COUSINS THOUGHT SHE WAS GETTING INTO MORE THAN SHE COULD HANDLE. THEY TOLD HER, "BEING A COP IS A MAN'S JOB." LAURA WASN'T AT ALL INFLUENCED BY HER FAMILY'S RESERVATIONS.

BY THE END OF 1954 SHE HAD REACHED HER GOAL AND WAS A POLICEWOMAN IN GOOD STANDING. ON THANKSGIVING OF THAT YEAR SHE TOLD HER PARENTS SHE WOULD BE LATE FOR THE FAMILY DINNER. AS THE EVENING WORE ON, THE FAMILY CELEBRATED WITHOUT HER. IDA LOUISE AND HER MOTHER FIXED A PLATE FOR LAURA AND SET IT ASIDE TO WARM WHEN SHE GOT HOME. OUTSIDE, RAIN BEGAN TO PELT DOWN, AND THE NIGHT SKY WAS BLACK.

FINALLY, AT ABOUT SEVEN OR EIGHT O'CLOCK, SHE DROVE IN. HER OLDER BROTHER WAS AT THE DOOR IMMEDIATELY. "WET AS A RIVER RAT," ONE OF THE OLD MEN REMARKED TO ANOTHER AS LAURA CAME INSIDE. IDA LOUISE HELPED HER WITH HER PACKAGES AND URGED HER TO SIT DOWN AND EAT.

"A LITTLE LATER, MOM," SHE SAID. AFTER CHANGING HER CLOTHES, SHE SAT DOWN ON THE COUCH CLOSE TO HER FATHER, WHO PUT HIS ARM AROUND HER. "HARD DAY?" HE ASKED. "I LIKE MY WORK, DAD," SHE TOLD HIM. "I FEEL LIKE I'M DOING SOMETHING WORTHWHILE."

HER FATHER KISSED HER IN RESPONSE.

From BEAUTY

There's beauty in the mystery
That fills a baby's eyes.
There's beauty in the love that gives
And feels no sacrifice.

There's beauty in the sweep of fields,
Dew-drenched and misty green;
There's beauty in the high-flung hills
With white clouds in between.

There's beauty in courageous souls
That would hard goals attain,
That rise with strength and fortitude
And sing with joy again.

PRISCILLA MAY MOORE
Best Loved Unity Poems

SAFE IN THE HEART OF OUR FAMILIES

*M*other and Aunt Mabel taught us children about the strength and safety one could find within the family. Mother believed that strong, healthy families are the cornerstones on which civilization is built. She talked about moral fiber, character growth, honor, and a sense of responsibility. Aunt Mabel never let us forget that we, the family, were in many ways one.

Harvesttime Pot Roast with Prunes and Homemade Noodles

4-POUND CHUCK OR RUMP ROAST	4 WHOLE CLOVES	
3 TABLESPOONS MARGARINE OR SHORTENING	2 TEASPOONS OR MORE SALT	
2 WINTER-KEEPING YELLOW ONIONS, SLICED	1 TEASPOON OR MORE BLACK PEPPER	
½ POUND UNCOOKED, PITTED PRUNES, SOAKED IN WARM WATER	1 CUP APPLE CIDER	
	HOMEMADE NOODLES (RECIPE FOLLOWS)	

MAKES 6 TO 8 SERVINGS

Wipe meat with a damp cloth.

In a large Dutch oven, over high heat, brown meat on all sides in hot fat. Add onions; sauté to a golden brown. Add prunes, seasonings, cider, and 1 cup water.

Reduce heat to low, cover, and simmer slowly until meat is tender, 3 or more hours. Check frequently and when necessary add more water. When meat is fork-tender, remove to a large platter. Cover lightly with a kitchen towel. Serve with buttered noodles.

Effie cooked beef until it got closer to Thanksgiving, then would whip out her holiday recipes and make a list of those she needed to perfect before taking them to the family feast. As soon as our menfolk knew she would be cookin' fancy dishes, they began to pester her. They'd ask her, "Thanksgivin's on its way, when are we going to get a chance to do a little sampling?"

Homemade Noodles

MAKES 6 OR MORE SERVINGS

2 EGGS, BEATEN TO A FROTH
2 TABLESPOONS MELTED BUTTER OR MARGARINE

3 TABLESPOONS HEAVY CREAM
½ TEASPOON LEMON JUICE
2 CUPS ALL-PURPOSE FLOUR

In a medium bowl combine eggs, butter, and cream soured with lemon juice until thick, about 5 minutes. Stir flour into egg-butter mixture. Slowly turn out onto a lightly floured surface; knead several times, then roll out very thin and cut into narrow strips. Cover with a clean kitchen towel until needed.

Bring a large pot of hot water or broth to a boil and drop noodles in. Boil until noodles are tender. Drain and serve or leave in broth and serve in large soup bowls.

Stuffed Acorn Squash

MAKES 4 SERVINGS

2 MEDIUM ACORN SQUASH
¾ POUND LEAN GROUND BEEF
1 SMALL ONION, DICED
¼ POUND MUENSTER CHEESE, SHREDDED

½ TEASPOON SUGAR
¼ CUP CATSUP
SALT AND PEPPER TO TASTE

Every year Mother's friend Lois raised a large patch of acorn squash. After the harvest, she created one special squash dish after another. She shared the recipes and squash with anyone who wanted them. The men in our family were all partial to this easy-to-

Cut each acorn squash lengthwise in half and discard seeds. Place squash halves cut side up in a 12-inch skillet. Add ½ inch water to skillet. Bring to a boil over high heat. Reduce heat to medium low. Cover skillet and cook until squash is fork-tender, about 10 minutes. Carefully drain liquid from squash cavities. Set aside.

In a large saucepan over high heat cook ground beef and onion until meat is browned and onion is tender, about 10 to 15 minutes. Stir occasionally. Add cheese, sugar, catsup, salt, and pepper, and stir to blend. Cook over low heat until cheese is melted; stir frequently.

To serve, place squash halves cut side up on a warm platter. Sprinkle lightly with additional salt and pepper as desired. Spoon meat mixture into squash cups. Serve immediately.

make stuffed squash. At our house it became a traditional Thanksgiving dish.

Mother's End-of-the-Season Cabbage Salad

2 CUPS CABBAGE, FINELY
 SHREDDED
1 SWEET RED PEPPER, CUT FINE

1 TEASPOON SALT
½ CUP SOUR CREAM DRESSING
 (RECIPE FOLLOWS)

MAKES 4 TO 6
SERVINGS

In a medium bowl combine cabbage, red pepper, and salt. Pour dressing over cabbage and mix well.

In the late fall, after large and medium cabbages have been harvested and the first rains come, the plants begin to grow a nest of baby cabbages that are tender and sweet. As they firm up Mother picks them and makes wintertime salads out of them.

Sour Cream Dressing

½ TEASPOON SALT
2 TEASPOONS SUGAR
PINCH OF CAYENNE (A VERY SMALL
 AMOUNT)

2 TEASPOONS LEMON JUICE
1 TEASPOON APPLE CIDER VINEGAR
½ CUP HEAVY CREAM

In a small bowl combine all ingredients. Mix thoroughly. Chill until ready to use. (For best flavor, make dressing just before assembling salad; refrigerate until vegetables are prepared and the meal is about to be served.)

Effie's Cranberry Apple Pie

MAKES ONE 9-INCH PIE

This tart and sweet pie is colorful and delicious. Those in our family who are fond of mincemeat pie also love this rich and tart cranberry-and-apple-filled pie.

FLAKY DOUBLE CRUST PASTRY (RECIPE FOLLOWS)
2 CUPS CRANBERRIES
1½ CUPS APPLES
1½ CUPS SUGAR
2 TABLESPOONS CORNSTARCH
¼ TEASPOON SALT
3 TABLESPOONS WATER
1 TABLESPOON MELTED BUTTER

Preheat oven to 450°F. Set out a 9-inch pie pan. Make pastry before preparing filling. Chill.

Wash cranberries; pare, core, and quarter apples. Thoroughly chop berries and apples and combine with sugar, cornstarch, salt, water, and melted butter.

Remove pastry from refrigerator. Divide dough into 2 portions, 1 slightly larger than the other. Form smaller portion into a ball and roll out on a floured surface. Line pan with pastry. Pour in filling. Roll out second portion and cut in 1½-inch strips. Weave pastry strips over top in a lattice design.

Bake at 450°F for 15 minutes; reduce temperature to 350°F and bake until crust is crisp and lightly browned and filling is cooked throughout, 30 minutes longer.

Flaky Double Crust Pastry

MAKES ONE 9-INCH PIE

2 CUPS ALL-PURPOSE FLOUR
1 TEASPOON SALT
¾ CUP COLD BUTTER OR MARGARINE
¼ CUP COLD WATER, MORE IF NEEDED
ABOUT 2 TABLESPOONS HEAVY CREAM (MILK MAY BE SUBSTITUTED)
SUGAR TO SPRINKLE ON TOP OF PIE

Into a medium bowl, sift flour and salt together. Cut in the butter until mixture resembles small peas. Sprinkle water over the mixture and mix with a fork until all particles cling together to form a ball. Roll out while fresh or chilled, as desired. Smooth cream over top crust. Lightly sprinkle with sugar.

SILENT PLACES

God, keep some silent places for us still,
Apart from those where man forever goes;
Some altars lit by sunset on the hill,
Or alcoves in the canyon wall, where glows
The crystal drop of moisture on the fern,
While ancient firs bend tenderly above,
For souls of men must sometimes deeply
    yearn
For silence such as this, to sense Thy love.

God, save them for us still, lest we forget —
These altars built eternities ago;
Mankind is prone to ruin, without regret,
Thy handiwork — oh, let it not be so!
The fret of all his petty self is seen
In masonry of towers and walls and piers,
But peace is in Thy murmuring forests
    green,
Thy peace, that shall abide throughout the
    years.

The clash and clang and roar of what he
    makes
Strikes to the nerves 'til man himself rebels;
But all Thy woodland minstrelsy awakes
Our better thoughts, and worship true
    compels;
Oh! may the towers of tall pines on the crest
Be temple signals, pointing out the way,
And in Thy silent places let us rest
A little while, sometimes, yea, rest and pray.

GRACE E. HALL

From WHERE BEAUTY ABIDES

Beauty escaped to the mountains high,
Aeons and aeons ago;
Her laughter re-echoing in the rills,
Mocking the littleness of man's ills,
Healing his soul with her magic thrills,
Aeons and aeons ago.

GRACE E. HALL
Patchwork

Silent Places

Although he's in his nineties, Uncle Ned still farms his great-grandfather's homestead, just as his grandfather and father before him had done. The lush fields, dressed faithfully with manure, have retained their fertility for nearly a hundred years. Field crops—sugar beets, potatoes, corn, and winter squashes—bear abundant crops, and cattle graze knee-deep in grasses. When asked about his farming, Uncle Ned talks about being a steward of the land.

Through the years as farming practices changed, he did not! As he put it, he never sprayed or polluted his God-given land with chemicals. Often he told young folks about his father and mother, who made a living on the family farm for ten children and themselves. And he would fondly tell about the nephews and grand-nephews who come over to help with spring planting and summer and fall harvests. He tells his friends that he's as healthy as a horse.

Often when some of the young folks go out to visit with him, they find the house and fields empty. They know from

J A N E   W A T S O N   H O P P I N G

EXPERIENCE THAT HE WILL BE OFF TO ONE OF GOD'S SILENT
PLACES, MORE THAN LIKELY UP ON THE MOUNTAIN IN HIS
DEARLY BELOVED WOODS. WHEN THE YOUNG ONES
QUESTION HIS SITTING ALONE IN THE NOVEMBER
COLD, HE TELLS THEM, "WHEN I'M UP HERE IN
THE TREES WITH THE FALLEN LEAVES AND
CRITTERS ABOUT ME, I FEEL LIKE I'M IN A
NATURAL CATHEDRAL. I THINK ABOUT MY
GREAT-GRANDPA AND THE LEGACY HE BOUGHT
FOR US WITH HIS OWN SWEAT. AND I THINK
ABOUT MOTHER AND THE CHILDREN."

ONE OR ANOTHER OF
THE YOUNG FOLK WILL COAX HIM TO THE HOUSE.
MARY, WHOM HE CALLED AN OLD BACHELOR'S
GRANDDAUGHTER, WOULD MAKE HOT TEA AND SET
OUT THE CAKE OR SWEET BREAD SHE HAD MADE FOR
HIM. AFTER ABOUT HALF AN HOUR OF LAUGHING AND
TALKING, THE YOUNG PEOPLE WOULD BID HIM GOOD-BYE.

AND, AS THEY LEFT, THE YOUNG FOLKS ALMOST ALWAYS FELT THAT
THEY CARRIED AWAY SOMETHING SPECIAL. MARY CALLED IT A GRAFTING OF INNER STRENGTH.
TODD, HER BOYFRIEND, CALLED IT PEACE WITH THE EARTH ABOUT ONE, AND OTHERS WHO HAD
CAME WITH MARY FOR THE FIRST TIME SPOKE OF A FEELING OF AWE IN UNCLE NED'S
PRESENCE.

Home Is Where the Heart Is

THROUGHOUT HIS LIFE, UNCLE BUD BORE THE SCARS OF THE 1929 DEPRESSION ON HIS HEART. MOST PARTICULARLY HE SORROWED OVER FRIENDS AND NEIGHBORS WHO HAD LOST EVERYTHING AND SUFFERED SO MUCH, AND HE GRIEVED FOR THE CHILDREN WHO, HE SAID, "NEVER SHOULD HAVE TO KNOW ABOUT SUCH THINGS."

AS HE GOT OLDER, HE MELLOWED SOME AND STOPPED RELIVING THE HARD TIMES. WHEN THINGS LOOKED BETTER, HE BOUGHT A USED TRACTOR AND A FEW HEAD OF WHITE-FACED CATTLE. AUNT SUE TOLD US ALL THAT HE WAS HIMSELF AGAIN.

HOWEVER, NONE OF US REALIZED JUST HOW DEEP HIS FEELINGS RAN, NOT UNTIL HIS GRANDSONS TOLD EVERYONE IN SCHOOL AND AT THE COUNTRY STORE THAT THEIR GRANDPA TALKED TO JESUS EVERY DAY, AND THAT HE THANKED GOD FOR NEIGHBORS WHO WERE NOW MAKING IT ALL RIGHT! MAE, AGE SEVEN, APPARENTLY TOLD HER PIANO TEACHER THAT SHE HAD HIDDEN BEHIND A CHAIR AND LISTENED WHILE HER GRANDFATHER CRIED WHEN HE TOLD GOD HOW WELL THE YOUNG CHILDREN HAD SURVIVED THE ORDEAL AND WHAT STRONG AND DECENT YOUNG MEN AND WOMEN THEY'D TURNED OUT TO BE.

LITTLE EDWARD WAITED UNTIL THE WHOLE FAMILY WAS ABOUT TO SIT DOWN TO A HARVEST GET-TOGETHER, THEN TOLD THE ASSEMBLED FAMILY THAT GRANDPA

EVEN THANKED GOD FOR THE PIGLETS AND THE HEIFERS. NOT TO BE OUTDONE, SUSIE ADVISED EVERYBODY THAT GRANDPA THANKED GOD FOR RAIN.

AUNT SUE APPARENTLY THOUGHT THIS "TELL ALL" WAS GOING TOO FAR AND SHE TOLD THE CHILDREN TO HUSH!

UNCLE BUD LAUGHED. HE TOLD AUNT SUE, "MAYBE IT WAS ABOUT TIME MY CHILDREN AND GRANDCHILDREN NEEDED TO KNOW THAT MANY A MAN IS GRATEFUL TO GOD FOR ALL THE WONDERFUL THINGS THAT MAKE HIS LIFE WORTH LIVING."

MANY BLESSINGS

Winter wraps around me, a coat of cold,
but between me and the winter, a coat of cloth,
heavy cloth and sheepskin, a mackinaw
keeping me warm inside the winter.

Between the barn and house I walk, crunching
*   snow*
beneath the toes of my boots.
Night wraps around me, blue-white and cold.
Ahead, in the house, a window warm and gold
holds promise of family and supper and rest.
In my mind I see the woodstove and hear it pop
with the sound of small logs burning; logs
*   that grew*
as trees on this farm; grew to be cut and keep
*   us warm;*
trees that knew my father and his father and
*   his.*

Father in heaven, accept my thanks
for these many blessings of winter, warmth,
*   cold*
and home; for hands and heart and family;
*   for bread*
and milk and eggs and meat; for this land.
Let me walk this land, I pray,
into the last sunset of my last day.
Let me leave it to my son
so he may feel, as I have done,
the glory of Your earth in its seasons;
in the awakening time of planting;
in the blaze of summer, in harvest,
in storing memories for the winter.

Thank you, Father, for these days,
for this night; for supper waiting
in warmth and light.

Amen.

ALVIN REISS

Index

Great-Grandma's beef pie, 104
green beans. *See* beans, green
green and yellow harvesttime snap
    bean salad with simple
    French dressing, 11
Grenville, R. H., xxiii, 75, 149
grouse, roast, 53
Guest, Edgar A., 133
Guetzlaff, Opal, 87, 145

H

Haas, Elizabeth Barr, vii
Hall, Grace E., xvii, 13, 58, 103,
    187
ham:
    ground, in upside-down
        cranberry meatloaf, 10
    processed baked, 158
hamburger heaven, easy-to-make,
    115
hard-cooked eggs, 77
Harvard beets, 26
"Harvest Festivals" (Hopping), 53
harvesttime fruit salad, 44
harvesttime pot roast with prunes
    and homemade noodles,
    183–84
a hearty supper soup, 30
herb buttered green beans, 124
"High Praise" (Crowell), 142
"Hither Come" (Smith and
    Bradbury), 51
"Hobgoblin Night" (Kuhn), 152
homemade buttermilk biscuit
    braid, 122–23
homemade chicken broth, 25
homemade croutons, 57
homemade noodles, 184
homemade tartar sauce, 84
homemade whole wheat crackers,
    31
hominy:
    au gratin, old-fashioned, 128–29
    old-fashioned cooked, 129
honey:
    baked apples, 100
    an' butter biscuits, 117
    candied yams, 92–93
    pecan pumpkin pie, 27
Hopping, Jane Watson, 53, 112
Hopping, Lula, 150
Hukill, Henry and Alma, 6
"Hunter's Moon" (Kuhn), 163

I

Ida Louise's braised chicken with
    vegetables, 24
Ida Louise's mashed sweet potato
    caramel, 169

"In the Lap of the Earth" (Kuhn),
    99
"In Thy Presence We Abide"
    (Reiss), 140

J

"Jack Frost" (Riley), 72
jelly roll cake, 151
Jerusalem artichokes, buttered, 106
"The Joy of Giving" (Adams), 28

K

Kamping, Alan, 6
Kamping, Herman and Vera, 6
Kamping, Loretta, 6
kedgeree, 85
Kuhn, Patricia Parish, 52, 67, 99,
    152, 159, 161, 163

L

"Laughing Song" (Riley), 8
leeks and potatoes au gratin, 9
lemon:
    biscuits, 81
    French dressing, 148
    sauce, a simple, 20
lemonade, easy-to-make, 137
lima beans. *See* beans, lima
"Limbs High Above Us" (Reiss),
    35–37
"The Little Red Ribbon" (Riley),
    viii
Longfellow, Henry Wadsworth,
    125

M

Maddox family, 6
Mae Dalton's roast turkey with
    sausage stuffing and golden
    glow gravy, 90–92
"Many Blessings" (Reiss), 191
maple syrup:
    about, 169
    in mashed sweet potato caramel,
        169
    popcorn balls, 51
"The Maple Tree" (Kuhn), 52
marmalade, citrus, a simple, 15
mayonnaise, whipped cream, 169
meatloaf, cranberry, upside-down,
    10
medium white sauce, 10, 78
milk punch, an old-time, 73
mincemeat cookies, harvest home,
    88
molasses, in shoofly pie, 12
Moore, Priscilla May, 182
"Morning Green to Twilight Gray"
    (Reiss), 39

Mother's end-of-the-season
    cabbage salad, 185
Mother's favorite sugar cookie, 136
Mother's harvest home mincemeat
    cookies, 88
Mother's moist roast beef with
    carrots, potatoes, and
    brown gravy, 138–39
Mother's potato refrigerator rolls,
    95
muffins:
    graham nut, 78
    see also biscuits

N

Newton, John, 108
Nightingale, Florence, 81
"No Blue Ribbon" (Kuhn), 159
noodles:
    in easy-to-make hamburger
        heaven, 115
    homemade, 184
Northern cornbread, 43
nut(s):
    date oatmeal bars, old-fashioned,
        114
    graham muffins, 78
    in pumpkin nutbread, 40
    vanilla frosting, 151
    see also individual names
nutbread, pumpkin, delicious, 40
nutmeg butter, broccoli with, 38

O

oatmeal:
    date-nut bars, old-fashioned, 114
    icebox cookies, 61
"Of Sun and Rain" (Guetzlaff), 145
"Old Homes" (Hall), 103
Old Land Place in Griffin Creek,
    xviii–xxiii
"The Old Trundle-Bed" (Riley), 34
old-country beef stew, 87
old-fashioned cream of pumpkin
    soup, 173
old-fashioned hominy au gratin,
    128–29
old-fashioned mashed potatoes, 175
old-fashioned pan fried brook
    trout, 20
old-fashioned steamed apples, 26
an old-time milk punch, 73
omelet, a simple French, 82
"On the Sunny Side" (Riley), 88
one crust apple pie, 124–25
one egg gingerbread, 32
onions, in a hearty supper soup, 30
orange(s):
    in citrus marmalade, a simple, 15

About the Author

I am rich in loved ones and have always been so. Our daughter, Colleen, lives nearby with her husband of ten years, Mark. Randy, our son, is working in construction and thus moves about the country. He calls home about every week or so, which keeps this mother's heart satisfied.

From childhood I have loved the earth about me: the wind and rain; hummingbirds; pinecones; acorns; squirrels; colored rocks and peacock feathers; trees and wildflowers; mountains, rivers, and lakes; fruits and vegetables right out of the garden; babies; lisping little ones; young fathers who love and care for their children, and mothers who teach them the lessons of life; old men and gentle old women; antiques; the past, present, and future—all of the abundant God-given gifts.